Is Healing For All?

by
Frederick K.C. Price

HARRISON HOUSE
Tulsa, Oklahoma

11th Printing
Over 100,000 in Print

Is Healing For All?
ISBN 0-89274-005-1
Copyright © 1976 by Frederick K.C. Price
Crenshaw Christian Center
P. O. Box 90000
Los Angeles, California 90009

Published by Harrison House, Inc.
P. O. Box 35035
Tulsa, Oklahoma 74153

Contents

Contents

1

Who or What Causes Sickness and Disease?

I want to ask you a question, a question that is in the hearts and minds of many people today. A question that is very seldom answered — I feel — in detail. A question that is very close to our hearts, because it deals with our very lives, our physical lives in this world and in this life. I want to ask that question and then I want to proceed, by the direction of the HOLY SPIRIT, by the written WORD OF GOD, to answer that question.

WE WILL ANSWER THE QUESTION BY THE WORD OF GOD.

We will not answer it by *my experience.* We will not answer it by *Theology.* We will not answer it by *Philosophy.* We will not answer it by *your experiences.* But we will answer this question *BY THE WRITTEN AND REVEALED WORD OF THE LIVING GOD.*

The question is this, "IS HEALING FOR ALL?" Is it God's will for every one of His *blood-bought* childern to be healed and walk in divine health? Is healing for everybody in the Body of Christ? Or is it God's will to *heal only some* and leave others *sick for His glory?* Or to make better people out of them?

IS HEALING FOR ALL?

Thousands upon thousands of people are afflicted and sick. Their lives are marred and racked with pain. Their effectiveness and efficiency in the Body of Christ have been drastically curtailed by debilitating disease. Is this God's will? Is it HIS DIVINE AND REVEALED PERFECT WILL for His Children to be sick?

Who or what causes sickness and disease?

Before we proceed with the answer to the question, "Is Healing For All?", we should first of all, I believe, establish these things. Where does sickness come from and who is behind sickness? Many people lay the blame for sickness, disease, and premature death upon the Heavenly Father. It hurts me in my heart when I hear them speak that way, because I know they are ignorant of the Word of God on that subject. Let's discover from the Bible. Let's not use anybody's experience. Let's not use what you think, what I think, what they say. Let's find out from the Bible.

The Apostle Peter is preaching here. He is speaking in the house of Cornelius, a Gentile man. He makes this very revealing declaration: *"How God anointed Jesus of Nazareth with the Holy Ghost and with power: who went about doing good, and healing all that were oppressed of the devil"* (Acts 10:38).

Now if I understand correctly, that verse is either saying that everybody Jesus healed was *satanically oppressed,* or else that verse didn't tell me all about the healing ministry of Jesus. It says He healed *all.* He didn't say all that were *possessed of the devil.* Peter said, *"healing all that were oppressed of the devil."*

If anybody should have known about the healing ministry of Jesus, Peter should have known. If anybody should have known what Jesus' attitude was concerning disease and sickness and it's origin, Peter should have known. Peter, James, and John were the BIG THREE. They were Jesus' right-hand men. They were in every high-level conference. When there was a major decision to make or truth to be revealed, Jesus would call aside Peter, James, and John.

For three and one-half years they walked with the Master. They heard the gracious words that fell from His lips. They watched the ministry of Jesus. And, on occasion, were sent out themselves under His auspices, to do the work that Jesus was doing.

Therefore, if anybody should have known what Jesus thought about sickness, and disease, Peter should have known.

Peter says that *"God anointed Jesus of Nazareth with the Holy Ghost and with power who went about doing good and healing all that were oppressed of the devil."*

I gather from *that* that SICKNESS IS SATANIC OPPRESSION.

We are establishing the origin of sickness, who is behind it. That is what we want to ascertain. Who *is* behind sickness? Is it Almighty God, our Heavenly Father, the God of love? Or is it *some other force, some other agency?*

Luke 13, beginning with verse 11, says, *"And, behold, there was a woman which had a spirit of infirmity eighteen years, and was bowed together, and could in no wise lift up herself, And when Jesus saw her, He called her to Him, and said unto her, Woman thou art loosed from thine infirmity. And he laid his hands on her: and immediately she was made straight, and glorified God."*

I would have you know — those of you who think that God puts you on the bed of affliction to get *glory* from you — that during all of those eighteen years this woman was bowed together and couldn't straighten herself up, it doesn't seem to indicate that she gave God *any glory.* But bless God! The moment she was made free, the first thing she did was give God glory! Not while she was bowed together, but when she was delivered!

Let's read on, in verse 14 it says, *"And the ruler of the synagogue answered with indignation, because that Jesus had healed on the sabbath day, and said unto the people, There are six days in which men ought to work: in them therefore come and be healed, and not on the sabbath day. The Lord then answered him, and said, thou hypocrite, doth not each of you on the sabbath loose his ox or his ass from the stall, and lead him away to watering? And ought not this woman, being a daughter of Abraham, whom Satan hath bound, lo, these eighteen years, be loosed from this bond on the sabbath day?"*

Jesus didn't say the Heavenly Father had her bound. He said Satan had her bound. And Jesus said because she was a *"daughter of Abraham"*, she ought to be *free.* And He proceeded to set her *FREE!*

I am perfectly convinced, from these two scriptures, that sickness and disease is of Satan — after all I am scriptural, because the Bible says that all you need is in the mouth of two or three witnesses, and I've given you two, so, I am *scripturally correct;* I may not be *theologically correct;* I may not be *denominationally correct;* and I may not be *traditionally correct,* but I could care less — *sickness is not of God.*

I am more interested in what the WORD OF GOD says, than what somebody's experience says. I am convinced that *sickness and disease is of Satan.* And I believe the above verses prove it.

Now, it is certainly true that if I don't live right, and I live out of the will of God, and I go out and do my own thing, then I am going to throw myself open for demonic oppression. Certainly that is true. I just can't sow my wild oats and be free from these attacks. But if I walk rightly, and if I walk in line with the Word of God, I am thoroughly convinced I can be free from sickness and disease.

If there is no *Gospel of healing,* why would anybody have faith for healing?

Paul very clearly declares that ". . . faith cometh by hearing and hearing by the Word of God" (Romans 10:17).

If we don't preach on it, and teach on it, faith for healing won't come. People won't be healed.

THERE IS A GOSPEL OF HEALING —

Now, let's go to another question. How does God heal the sick?

Again, we appeal to the authority of the Word of God.

PROVERBS 4:20-22:
20. My son, attend to my words; incline thine ear unto my sayings.
21. Let them (my words) not depart from thine eyes; keep them in the midst of thine heart. (Why God?)
22. For they are life unto those that find them and health to all their flesh.

That word, *health,* in the Hebrew literally means *medicine,* or *healing.* THIS WORD IS GOD'S MEDICINE.

He said, *"for they"* (my words) *"are life to those that find them,"* (and my words — my words) *"are health to all their flesh"* (*medicine* to all their flesh).

Praise God! If I take God's medicine, I'll be free from sickness!

"IS HEALING FOR ALL?

How does God heal the sick? *"My son attend to my words."*

Why? *"MY WORDS ARE HEALTH."*

All right, let's look at another passage of Scripture. *"He sent His Word and healed them, and delivered them from their destructions"* (*Psalm 107:20*). In other words, The WORD OF GOD IS A HEALING WORD.

Now let's read the first verse of the Gospel of JOHN, the first chapter . . . *"In the beginning was the Word, and the Word was with God, and the Word was God."* If you look down in the 14th verse of that same chapter, it says, *"And the Word was made flesh, and dwelt among us."*

What did the *Word* do?

The Word was made flesh and *the Word dwelt among us.*

What did the *Word do* when He dwelt among us?

"He went about doing good and healing all that were oppressed of the devil" (Acts 10:38).

The following Scripture says, *"Jesus Christ the same yesterday, and today, and for ever"* (*Hebrews 13:8*). If Jesus was the healing Word yesterday, He has to be the healing Word today, and He will be the healing Word tomorrow, or else He is not "the same yesterday, today, and forever."

"Well," somebody says, "What about Job?"

What about Job?

"Didn't God afflict Job? Didn't God test Job?"

No.

"No?"

You remember the story in the first chapter of the Book of Job. Let's punch some holes in the *balloons* of some false teaching and some false doctrine. I'll paraphrase, "The sons of God came unto God, and Satan was in the midst, and God said, 'Where have you been?' and Satan said, 'I have been walking to and fro in the earth, and walking up and down in it.' God said, 'Have you considered my servant Job?' And Satan said, Yeah, I've been watching him closely, but you have built a hedge around him. I can't get to him, that hedge is up there. But if you will pull the hedge down, I will make him curse you to your face'."

You see, Satan tried to get God to pull the hedge down. Now let's read verse 12, *"And the Lord said unto Satan, 'Behold, (look — see) all that he hath is in thy power'."*

Satan didn't even know that the hedge was down.

Job had pulled the hedge down. JOB HAD PULLED IT DOWN.

You say, "Well, God permitted Satan to afflict Job."

Sure He did, just like He permitted Adam to sin, but He told that *dummy,* "Don't do it."

Permission is not commission. We are free moral agents. God doesn't have us on a string like a puppet. *He gives us free will.*

He said to that *silly* Adam, "Man, don't do it. In the day that you do it, you will surely die." (He didn't say you *might* die.) So — Adam went right out and did it. Ate of the forbidden fruit. That's why I call him dumb. THAT IS DUMB!

If you said to me, "There are three roaring lions outside that haven't eaten in seven days. Fred, don't go out that door!", and I go out that door and the lions eat me—THAT'S DUMB!

Satan started afflicting Job. The news started coming in; nothing but bad news, one servant after another, bad news on top of bad news.

Let's go over to the 20th verse and see what Job did. *"Then Job arose, and rent his mantle, and shaved his head, and fell down upon the ground, and worshipped. And said, Naked came I out of my mother's womb, and naked shall I return thither: the Lord gave, and the Lord hath taken away; blessed be the name of Lord."*

"The Lord gave and the Lord hath taken away" is not a true statement. God didn't do that to Job. Satan did it. But Job thought that God did it. Just like we have been thinking, "Well — the *will of the Lord be done.* The Lord has plucked His little flower from the earth and put it up in His heavenly garden, in Heaven. The Lord has given and the Lord has taken away, blessed be the name of the Lord."

Remember what we read in the first part of that chapter. God didn't take those things away from Job. *Satan took them.*

Job didn't rashly accuse God, but he didn't know anybody else to *put it on,* so he said the Lord did it.

Sure — God permitted it, because Job was a free moral agent.

As long as Job walked in *faith,* the wall — the hedge — was *up.* But when he started walking in *unbelief* and *doubt* the hedge was pulled down. JOB PULLED IT DOWN.

"Be sober, be vigilant; because your adversary the devil, as a roaring lion, walketh about, seeking whom he may devour" (I Peter 5:8).

Remember, Jesus said, and this is a principle that pertains at all times in the universe in the scheme of things with God, *"For verily I say unto you that whosoever shall say unto this mountain, Be thou removed, and be thou cast into the sea; and shall not doubt in his heart, but shall believe that those things which he saith shall come to pass; he shall have whatsoever he saith"* (Mark 11: 23). Not what he *believes*, but he'll have what he *says*. "WHATSOEVER HE SAITH."

We've missed that. Now watch this. Job had what he said. *"For the thing which I greatly feared is come upon me . . ." (Job 3:25).* Job brought it upon himself. HE HAD WHAT HE SAID.

As you read the book of Job, you found that it has 42 chapters. You think you're reading the whole lifetime of Job. Hebrew scholars tell us that the entire book of Job transpired in nine to twelve months. This wasn't a man's whole lifetime spent being sick and afflicted. It was from nine to twelve months, at the most.

If you will scrutinize the book very carefully, you will find that Job wasn't trying to *get his healing* all of that nine months. The moment that Job got back in faith and *prayed for his three friends*, he was delivered. THAT'S THE WORD OF GOD, my friends!

"And the Lord turned the captivity of Job, when he prayed for his friends: also the Lord gave Job twice as much as he had before" (Job 42:10).

"You mean to tell me that God had taken Job *captive?*"
It says — "GOD TURNED HIS CAPTIVITY."
Who was he *in captivity* to?
Satan.

When Job got *back in faith*, stopped messing around and accusing God, saying, *"I wish the day had never come when my mother and father came together,"* and all that other *mess*, and after God called him on the carpet and said, *"stand up here, gird yourself up. Where were you when I laid the foundations of the earth, where were you when the morning stars sang together and the sons of God shouted for joy? Where were you?"* *(Job 38:3-7).*

That hushed Job's mouth. He turned and got back in faith and God immediately delivered him.

If you read the rest of the book, you know that God gave Job twice as much of everything that he had before. He had the same number of children, and the Bible says — bless God Almighty! — that Job lived 140 more years. That doesn't sound like a man who was sick and afflicted all of his lifetime. He lived 140 more years. Praise God!

All right, somebody says, "Yeah — but what about Paul's thorn? Wasn't Paul sick? Didn't he pray three times and God told him to keep his sickness? Didn't he have bad eyes, and a bad back, and a bad foot, and a bad this, and a bad that?"

No!

"No?"

I'm just reading the Bible, friends! Have you noticed that my name didn't appear in any of the Bible verses we've read?

"And lest I should be exalted above measure through the abundance of the revelations, there was given to me a thorn in the flesh, (Paul didn't say 'God gave it to him') *the messenger of Satan to buffet me lest I should be exalted above measure"* *(II Corinthians 12:7).*

Now that was Paul's estimate of the situation. God didn't tell him that He gave him that to keep him *humble,* but Paul was a man who was prone to brag and boast. Therefore he took it upon himself to believe all of this that was coming upon him was going to help him to stay humble.

GOOD NEWS FOR MODERN MAN says, *"he was sick with a painful physical ailment."* That statement *is not in the Greek.* That was added by some man, based on *his* experience. *AND WE SWALLOW THAT STUFF HOOK, LINE, SINKER, FISHING-POLE, THE REEL, THE FISHERMAN, AND HIS BOOTS.* We swallow the whole *dumb* thing.

Paul tells you right there in that 7th verse *what it was.* He says, *"the messenger of Satan."* If you read that in the Greek, the word, messenger, is *angelos,* from which we derive the English word *angel.* It was one of Satan's angels sent to harass and bug him. If you read Paul's life, you'll see that he was harassed and bugged the whole time through.

When Paul prayed, God said, *"my grace is sufficient."* Sure, His grace is sufficient. Do you know what the *grace of God* is? *THE AUTHORITY TO USE THE NAME OF JESUS.*

James 5:7 says, *"Resist the Devil and he will flee from you."* God isn't going to take Satan and demons out of here, yet.

They have a *time* set, but in the meantime He has given the Church authority over Satan. *BUT, IF YOU DON'T RESIST HIM, HE WON'T FLEE FROM YOU.* Because, don't you realize that if Paul prayed three times, if he was, *in fact* physically sick, and God said for him to remain sick, do you realize that would be the first time in the whole Bible where God *ever* told anybody to keep their sickness? That by virtue of itself would invalidate the Bible. Because in more than one place, it says, *"God is no respector of persons."* (Romans 2:11, Ephesians 6:9, Colossians 3:25).

If that's not respecting persons, I don't know what is.

Paul goes on to say, *"a thorn in the flesh to buffet me."*

The literal meaning of the word, *buffet*, means to strike with the hand or with the fist. It means a repeated striking-striking-striking. A good illustration is a ship at anchor in the harbor, with the waves slapping against the sides 24 hours a day. That would mean that Paul was sick all of his lifetime. And I'm telling you, if a man who was afflicted and sick all of his lifetime could write more than half the New Testament, establish all of the churches he established, live out a full life, and came to the end and didn't say that they took his life, but instead he said, *"I've fought a good fight, I've finished my course."* If he could do all of that while he was afflicted with sickness, then we ought to pray to get the same thing Paul had so we could do half as much as he did!

Just think of all the Christians, bless their dear hearts, (and my heart goes out to them when I see this happen) who are letting Satan get the advantage over them. They — the Body of Christ — have been laid flat on their backs, and didn't even get started on their course.

Whatever was wrong with Paul didn't stop him from doing the will of God and getting the job done. Isn't that right?

Praise the name of the Lord!*

Someone else asks, "Well — what about the man born blind? Didn't Jesus say that he was sick for the glory of God?"

No! Let's read some more Scripture.

John 9:1-4

1 And as Jesus passed by, he saw a man which was blind from his birth.

2 And his disciples asked him, saying, Master, who did sin, this man, or his parents, that he was born blind?

3 Jesus answered, Neither hath this man sinned, nor his parents: but that the works of God should be made manifest in him.

4 I must work the works of Him that sent me . . .

The Jews believed that a baby could sin in its mother's womb. Jesus told them that neither the parents nor the man had done any particular thing to cause him to be born blind.

Here, you see, we get into a dilemma. Because you must realize that in the original Greek language in which the original manuscripts were written everything was written in capital letters. There were no small case letters, no punctuation marks, and no verse or chapter divisions. These were added by the translators as reference points, and as best they could determine to give sense to the meaning.

Now without changing any of the words, I am going to change only some punctuation marks merely for your consideration. You are under no obligation to accept this. But I would suggest it to you. Let's read the same Scripture again:

JOHN 9:1-2 KJV (Punctuation by Price)

And as Jesus passed by (comma), he saw a man which was blind from his birth (period).

And his disciples asked him (comma), saying (comma), Master (comma), who did sin (comma), this man (comma), or his parents (comma), that he was born blind (question mark)?

*Paul's thorn is explained in greater detail in Chapter 2.

His disciples asked Jesus a simple question — a two-fold question. They knew the man was blind and they wanted to know what caused it. Did the man sin? Or did his parents sin?

That is going to elicit from Jesus one of three answers: (a) the parents, (b) the man, (c) neither.

Let's read on:

JOHN 9:3-4 KJV (Punctuation and comments by Price)

Jesus answered (comma), Neither hath this man sinned (comma), nor his parents (period). (When Jesus said "Neither" that answered the question didn't it?) (*Capital B*) But that the works of God should be manifest in him (comma), I must work the works of Him that sent me. . . ."

Then Jesus proceeded to do the works! He spat on the ground. He made some clay. He anointed his eyes. He sent him to the pool of Siloam. The man washed and came seeing! Glory to God! Jesus didn't say that the man was born blind "for the glory of God".

Certainly blindness is here because sin is in the world. All bad things are here in the world because of sin, but the parents nor the man had done nothing specific to cause the man to be born blind. But Jesus said, "BUT THAT THE WORKS OF GOD SHOULD BE MADE MANIFEST IN HIM (COMMA), I MUST DO THOSE WORKS." In other words, "If I don't do them, they won't be done in him." Then He proceeded to do them.

Now you don't have to accept that, but doesn't it kind of change things when you just make those little corrections?*

Now remember this, Jesus was the will of God in action. *"For I came down from heaven, not to do mine own will, but the will of Him that sent me"* (John 6:38). That meant that He came down from heaven, not to do His own will but the will of who? the Father!

All right, let's read some more: *"Jesus saith unto him, Have I been so long time with you, and yet hast thou not known me, Phillip? He that hath seen me hath seen the*

---

*Read Lamsa's translation of the New Testament concerning this verse. I think it will be an eye opener for you.

Father; and how sayest thou then, Show us the Father? Be-
lievest thou not that I am in the Father, and the Father in
me? the words that I speak unto you I speak not of myself:
but the Father that dwelleth in me, he doeth the works."
(John 14:9-10).

How did the father dwell in Jesus? By the anointing of
the Holy Spirit. *"How God anointed Jesus of Nazareth with*
the Holy Ghost and with power: who went about doing good,
and healing all that were oppressed of the devil" (Acts
10:38).

Jesus never did claim to heal anybody. He said, ". . . *The*
Father that dwelleth in me, He doeth the works" (John
14:10).

Well now, don't you know that if the *Father in Him* did
the works, it must have been the *will of the Father,* to do the
works? So that must have meant that it was *God's will* for
those people to be well.

I want to propose another question as we go along. Suppose God *is* a respecter of persons, and it *is* His *divine de-*
creed will to heal only some people, and not everybody; how
did the people in the day in which Jesus lived know which
people to bring to Jesus for healing?

Did they go down the line and say, "Yeah it's His will
to heal him; not her, him — yes, her — no, her — yes, not
him"? How did they know? Let's find out how they knew
which sick people to bring to Jesus for healing, since as
some tell us, it's not God's will to heal *all!*

"IS HEALING FOR ALL?"

"And Jesus went about all Galilee, teaching in their
synagogues, and preaching the gospel of the kingdom, and
healing all manner of sickness and all manner of disease
among the people" (Matthew 4:23).

Not some manner of sickness and some manner of
disease, but all of it.

Matthew 8:16-17:

16. When the even was come, they brought unto Him
many that were possessed with devils: and He cast out
the spirits with his word, and healed all that were sick.
17. That it might be fulfilled which was spoken by
Esaias the prophet, saying, Himself took our infirmities
and bare our sicknesses.

". . . He cast out the spirits with His Word, and (healed some that were sick — a few — the worst cases?) HE HEALED *THEM ALL THAT WERE SICK.*" Verse 17 tells us why, *"That it might be fulfilled which was spoken by Esaias, the prophet, saying Himself took our infirmities and bare our sicknesses."*

The word *infirmities* is actually the word *sicknesses,* and the word *sicknesses* is actually *diseases.*

Did you notice that they brought everybody, and isn't that something! He went on and healed them anyhow! Poor Jesus didn't know that it wasn't God's will to heal everybody, and He went on and healed them anyhow! And yet He said He always did the thing that pleased His Father. He said it wasn't even Him doing the works, "But the Father in Him."

Do you think that even God didn't know that He wasn't supposed to heal everybody? Because, *IN THAT CROWD THEY ALL GOT HEALED! THAT WAS THE WILL OF THE FATHER!*

"Wasn't He supposed to leave some *sick for His glory?"* No! Praise God!

Matthew 9:35; 10:1:
35 And Jesus went about all the cities and villages, teaching in their synagogues, and preaching the gospel of the kingdom, and healing every sickness and every disease among the people.
36 But when He saw the multitudes He was moved with compassion on them, because they fainted, and were scattered abroad, as sheep having no shepherd.
37 Then saith He unto his disciples, The harvest truly is plenteous, but the laborers are few: Pray ye therefore the Lord of the harvest, that he will send forth laborers into his harvest.
10:1 And when he had called unto him his twelve disciples, he gave them power (the word power in the Greek is the word *exousia,* which means authority, or right) against unclean spirits, to cast them out, and to heal all manner of sickness and all manner of disease.

Look at verse 35 again. It says, *"that He healed every sickness and every disease among the people."* Now I would believe, if he said every sickness and every disease, that He healed everybody. I think that is a safe assumption.

"But when Jesus knew it, he withdrew himself from thence: and great multitudes followed him and He healed them all" (Matthew 12:15).

Now in the 14th Chapter of Matthew, we will read verse 14 first, *"And Jesus went forth, and saw a great multitude, and was moved with compassion toward them, and He healed their sick."*

Well, if I understand English, it would seem to me that what it is saying is that He healed *all* the sick people in that multitude, isn't that right?

Let's stay in this same chapter. *"And when they were gone over, they came into the land of Gennesaret. And when the men of that place had knowledge of him, they sent out into all that country round about, and brought unto him all that were diseased;* (not some, but *all* that were diseased) *and besought him that they might only touch the hem of his garment; and as many as touched were made perfectly whole"* (Matthew 14:34-36).

That means everybody who touched Him got healed. Is that right? You know Jesus did say, *"if ye continue in my word, then are ye my disciples, indeed: And ye shall know the truth, and the truth shall make you free"* (John 8:31-32). THE TRUTH SHALL MAKE YOU FREE!

Let's read, *"Now when the sun was setting, all they that had any sick with divers diseases brought them unto him; and he laid his hands on every one of them, and healed them"* (Luke 4:40).

I'm telling you, God is messing up *our* theology. He's healing everybody! Isn't He supposed to leave some of them *sick for His glory?*

Luke   6:17-19:
17 And he came down with them, and stood in the plain, and the company of his disciples, and a great multitude of people out of all Judea and Jerusalem, and from the sea coast of Tyre and Sidon, which came to hear him, and to be healed of their diseases;
18 And they that were vexed with unclean spirits: and they were healed.

19 And the whole multitude sought to touch him: for there went virtue out of him, and healed *them all.*

Please remember that we proposed a question. "If God were a respector of persons and willed to heal only some and not everybody, how were the people in the day in which Jesus lived to know which ones to bring?

Apparently, they didn't know any better, because He healed every one of them. Now notice in all of these Scriptures, they brought *all.* Notice also this very important fact. Everybody that Jesus healed was living under the OLD COVENANT DISPENSATION. Under the old covenant, and every one of them got healed.

Let's read on, *"But now hath he obtained a more excellent ministry, by how much also he is the mediator of a better covenant, which was established upon better promises:* (Hebrews 8:6). If we have a better covenant, established on better promises, better than the old covenant, and everybody under the old covenant got healed, why can't I get healed under the new covenant? I'm supposed to have a better covenant. Is the new one better than the old one?

Praise God! It is better.

Now — you decide — "IS HEALING FOR ALL?"

If healing is not for everyone, then what are we to do with such Scriptures as Matthew 8:17, which says, *". . . Himself took our infirmities, and bore our sicknesses"?*

What are we to do with I Peter 2:24, which says, *". . . with his stripes ye were healed"?* (Ye who? Ye who are in the body of Christ.) If I understand my Bible correctly, it says, "with His stripes I was healed." That means I am healed, doesn't it? DOESN'T IT?

James 5:14-15:

14 Is any sick among you? let him call for the elders of the church; and let them pray over him, anointing him with oil in the name of the Lord:

15 And the prayer of faith shall save the sick, and the Lord shall raise him up; . . .

"Is any sick" (Is any sick—is any sick — man—woman— boy — girl — black — white — old— young — educated — ignorant?) *"Is any sick among you, let him call for the elders of the church; and let them pray over him, anointing him with oil, in the name of the Lord: And the prayer of faith*

shall SAVE THE SICK AND THE LORD SHALL RAISE HIM UP." Who? Any that's sick, that's who!

"IS HEALING FOR ALL?"

Well, I'll tell you one thing for sure. Healing sure is for me. If nobody else on the face of PLANET EARTH ever gets healed, Frederick K. C. Price will be healed. I believe that.

Sickness is a curse of the law. Read the 28th chapter of Deuteronomy. It covers every disease known to mankind. It is the *curse* for breaking God's law. Poverty is a part of the curse of the law, too.

But — bless God! Let's read these startling and astounding words. *"Christ hath redeemed us from the curse of the Law, being made a curse for us . . . That the blessing of Abraham might come on the Gentiles through Jesus Christ . . ." (Galatians 3:11-14).*

I'm not under the *curse.* I'm not under sickness and disease. So — I just refuse to accept it.

Oh yes — Satan and demons try to bring symptoms on my body, don't misunderstand me. I'm not saying that I'm not attacked. I'm not saying that Satan doesn't *try* to put it on me. I'm just saying, *"I NEVER SIGN FOR THE PACK-AGE!"*

I tell him to "get thee hence, Satan, in the Name of Jesus!"

We don't allow sickness in our home. I have a young daughter, whenever something attacks her, the first thing she does is find Mother or Father, and says, "Lay hands on me, and I'll be healed."

We *lay hands* on her and *it* goes.

She goes on back and starts playing and forgets all about it.

"IS HEALING FOR ALL?"

Satan will try to attack you; if you are fool enough to accept it, he'll put it on you.

I believe that the Scriptures *conclusively* prove that it is so.

"HEALING IS FOR ALL!"

PRAISE GOD!

2

Paul's Thorn

I have often said, "You as a Christian cannot believe beyond your actual knowledge of God's Word concerning any particular subject."

You cannot believe to receive the Holy Spirit, if you do not know it's God's will to give you the Holy Spirit. You cannot believe for miracles if you have not been made aware, by the Word of God, that God is still a miracle worker today. You can't believe unless you have actual knowledge concerning these subject areas.

Neither can you believe for healing for your body, unless you (first of all) know that it's God's will to heal you. In other words, you cannot exercise faith to receive anything from God until you know that it's His will to give it to you. You can't believe for *what you don't know you can have*. The only way you can know it is to *HEAR THE WORD OF GOD* on it.

One morning, in one of our Bible classes, I asked this question. "How many of you have ever heard a sermon on *divine healing?* (Now, we have a cross-section of many denominations here, Baptist, Methodist, Presbyterian, Lutheran, Catholic, and many others. Many of them had been in these several denominations for ten years or more.)

I went on to say, "Now, I don't mean that you haven't heard the fact that somebody said that God is able to do anything, *that kind of thing,* or perhaps you heard that God *could heal,* but you've never actually heard an entire message based on the *Word of God* on the fact that it is *God's will to heal,* that God will heal today, and that He will heal you."

Not one single person, Baptist, Presbyterian, Methodist, Catholic, (there was even a Congregationalist lady there that day) had ever heard a sermon on *divine healing.*

Is it any wonder that many people in these denominations don't believe in these things? They don't believe it because they've never heard it. I don't care how sincere you

are or how educated or uneducated you are academically
speaking, you cannot believe beyond your actual knowledge
of God's Word.

That's why it's so important to get this *Word* built into
you. Some people give lip service to it and that's all. They
intellectually assent and agree that the Bible *is* true, but they
don't realize that they're not believing God. They say —
mentally assenting — that the Bible is true, that it does say
that in there, and "I believe that." But they don't ACT ON
THAT — so — they never receive healing for themselves.
Then they count themselves to be one of those who it's *"not
God's will to heal."*

That's sad, because it's a deception and a delusion of
Satan.

One of the cardinal reasons that many people do not
believe in divine healing is because they have heard so much
negativism about it all of their lives. They may not have
heard a sermon on *divine healing*, but they have heard about
the fact that *"It is not God's will to heal everybody,"* and that
when you pray for people you must pray, *"if it be thy will,"*
and of course if the person dies, that meant it *wasn't His will*
to heal him.

YOU DID EVERYTHING?

Some say, "Oh — I know it's so — but I tried it and it
didn't work for me."

Well, even God said, *"Put me in remembrance . . ."*
(Isaiah 43:26). So we have to go over and over these things
until they get past that *"PEA"* that's sitting between your
shoulder-blades and gets down into your spirit, so you can
start *believing it.*

"But I did everything you told me, and it still didn't
work. I suppose I'm one of those *it isn't God's will to heal."*

Well, I'm frank to tell you, that if it didn't work for you,
then you didn't do what God said, and if you say you did
what God said and you didn't get it, you're mistaken about it.

IT WORKS — friends! This Book — God's Word —
works. Glory to God!

If it doesn't work, then salvation doesn't work, prayer
doesn't work, forgiveness doesn't work, righteousness doesn't
work, redemption doesn't work, and there's going to be no

Resurrection — and there's no Heaven, no hell, no Judgment Day, and Jesus is not coming back again.

If it didn't work for you, I'm quick to tell you, if you say you've done what God said and you didn't get your healing, you're mistaken, because *He said you'd get it.*

I've done many things, and I just knew I was right. I knew I was doing it right, then I found out I was in the wrong place, at the wrong time, with the wrong people. But I thought I was right.

You can do the *wrong thing* with the *right intention.*

One of the things that *hangs people up,* relative to divine healing, is "PAUL'S THORN IN THE FLESH."

Everywhere I go to minister to people, if I'm ministering the *Word* and I'm talking about healing, everytime I say, "Are there any questions?" two questions always *come up.*

"What about Paul's thorn? and "What about Job?"

We talked about both Job and Paul's thorn in Chapter One of this book, but let's probe a little deeper into the subject of "PAUL'S THORN," not only for your sake, but also so you can minister to other people, so you can help them to *see the light.*

Satan is a very clever deceiver. He has deceived the vast majority of Christians into believing that *it's not God's* will for them to have good health, that it's not God's will for them to walk free from sickness and disease, but rather, God wants them sick and afflicted, because He's using that to make a better person out of them.

People really believe that. They're saying, "Look at me, I have double cancer. They can't cure it. They sent me home to die. I'm something special, I'm one of God's *elect.*"

That is religious pride.

"God's not going to heal me because I'm one of His special ones — I have tuberculosis –- it's not everybody that has T.B."

Anybody can be sick, don't you know that. You don't have to do a thing. It takes something to stand against disease and sickness when Satan brings it against you. Just drop your guard, you'll be sick sooner or later.

II Corinthians 12:1-10:

1 It is not expedient for me doubtless to glory. I will come to visions and revelations of the Lord.

2 I knew a man in Christ above fourteen years ago, (whether in the body, I cannot tell; or whether out of the body, I cannot tell: God knoweth;) such an one caught up to the third heaven.

3 And I knew such a man, (whether in the body, or out of the body, I cannot tell: God knoweth;)

4 How that he was caught up into paradise, and heard unspeakable words, which is not lawful for a man to utter.

5 Of such an one will I glory: yet of myself I will not glory but in mine infirmities.

6 For though I would desire to glory, I shall not be a fool! for I will say the truth: but now I forbear, lest any man should think of me above that which he seeth me to be, or that he heareth of me.

7 And lest I should be exalted above measure through the abundance of the revelations, there was given to me a thorn in the flesh, the messenger of Satan to buffet me, lest I should be exalted above measure.

8 For this one thing I besought the Lord thrice, that it might depart from me.

9 And he said unto me, My grace is sufficient for thee: for my strength is made perfect in weakness. Most gladly therefore will I rather glory in my infirmities, that the power of Christ may rest upon me.

10 Therefore I take pleasure in infirmities, in reproaches, in necessities, in persecutions, in distresses for Christ's sake: for when I am weak, then am I strong.

Now we're going to qualify some of these words. Notice that Paul says, "there was given to me a thorn in the flesh." Now he didn't say, *God gave me a thorn in the flesh.* He said, *"there was given to me a thorn in the flesh."* Paul apparently, based upon the WORD, was a man who was very prone to boasting about what a great individual he was. So he thought the "thorn" was given to him to keep him humble.

Some people say that "the thorn in Paul's flesh" was a bad back, or bad feet, bad eyes, or something else was wrong with him.

In fact the translation of the Bible called *"GOOD NEWS FOR MODERN MAN"* says in II Corinthians 12:7, "there was given to Paul a painful physical ailment."

Now I read and studied that Scripture in the "Greek"; that's not in there. That is one of Satan's cleverest traps for Christians.

Now I can understand why they translate it like that. When you are in one of those denominations that doesn't believe in divine healing, and *divine healing* is not preached, you don't know about it. (I don't mean to imply by any stretch of the imagination that they don't love the Lord. There are just as good Christians in the Baptist, or Methodist, or Catholic churches, and they are born-again and on their way to heaven.)

They go out and pray for somebody, and after a while they pray for about five people and they all die. They finally come to the conclusion that it must not be God's will to heal everybody. Then they start changing their prayers to, *"Lord if it be thy will, heal them,"* and sure enough they all die, because that's not a prayer of faith. That's a prayer of doubt. ". . . If it's your will" means you don't know whether it's His will or not. That prayer is doomed to failure; as soon as it comes out of your mouth, it falls on the floor. It doesn't even get out of the room, because it's a prayer of doubt.

Jesus said to the woman with the issue of blood, (and to us too) "your faith has made you whole," not *your doubt.*

So what happens when they come around to translating the Bible is, they pick these Scriptures out and in order to justify the *experiences* that they have had, they look at Paul and say, "well — surely -- that thorn must have been a sickness!"

Then they use *their experiences* to validate that rather than the SPIRIT OF GOD to give them the revelation of it, so they put in there, "a painful, physical ailment".

Then when they go and pray for somebody and the person succumbs, they have an out. When the relatives come around and they wonder why the guy died, they *very cleverly* pick the Bible up and say, "Well after all you know, Jim wasn't nearly as good as Paul, and after all the Lord let Paul be sick all of his life — so, if Paul was sick you might as well accept yours and don't worry about it!"

See what I mean?

I believe the Bible means what it says, except where words are not translated properly. Many times these words are not translated properly. Many times (it's not an incorrect translation in that it's giving you something that's not in there.) it's just not giving you the FULLNESS OF THE TRANSLATION — so you don't get the FULL meaning. That is why you need to do a lot of studying to get it.

I want to know what the Bible says — myself.

"IS HEALING FOR ALL?"

Now if my Father didn't mean it, then He told me a fairytale, but I believe Him. He said that with Jesus' stripes *I WAS HEALED. SO* — if *I WAS* — *I AM* and if *I AM* — *I IS!* It's just as simple as that.

If you don't think sickness is prevalent, if you don't think it's necessary to talk about disease, sickness, and healing, listen to this. I looked in the yellow pages of the telephone book, and I counted 249 hospitals in Los Angeles. And I may have missed some. Brother! That's a lot of hospitals, and they are building more every day, and they don't have enough beds for all the people in the hospitals they have now.

Many of those people are Christians, the *Body of Christ*, flat on their backs. Satan has the advantage over them.

Let's read some Scriptural references about this business of *"thorns"* in the OLD TESTAMENT and see if we can find anything that we can use as a guideline to determine if the *thorn* that Paul had, was — in fact — a physical, painful ailment or sickness — or is *that something that man has attached to it.*

Numbers 33:50-55:

50 And the Lord spake unto Moses in the plains of Moab by Jordan near Jericho, saying,

51 Speak unto the children of Israel, and say unto them, When ye are passed into the land of Canaan;

52 Then ye shall drive out all the inhabitants of the land from before you, and destroy all their pictures, and destroy all their molten images, and quite pluck down all their high places:

53 And ye shall dispossess the inhabitants of the land, and dwell therein: for I have given you the land to possess it.

54 And ye shall divide the land by lot for an inheritance among your families; and to the more ye shall give the more inheritance, and to the fewer ye shall give the less

inheritance: every man's inheritance shall be in the place where his lot falleth; according to the tribes of your fathers ye shall inherit.

55 But if ye will not drive out the inhabitants of the land from before you; then it shall come to pass, (that those — that those) that those which ye let remain shall be pricks in your eyes, and *thorns in your sides,* and shall vex you in the land wherein ye dwell.

Now, how interpretest *thou?* You interpret. What is it saying?

What does it mean?

Let's see if we can get a *consensus* of opinion.

I believe that He is telling them that if they don't get rid of those people, they will be an irritant (just as a *prick* is an irritant to your body) to them.

Have you ever had a hair fall out of your head (or an eyelash) and get into your eye? It's almost like somebody hit you. Have you ever had a speck of dust or something get in your eye? It's just like somebody hit you with something. Have you ever been walking out in the woods, and you got a prick or thorn from a bush in your side, or in your clothes, or in your socks? You couldn't find it right away, and every time you moved that thing was an *irritation to you.*

He was using that statement *metaphorically.* Meaning that, just as a *thorn-in-the-side,* and a *prick-in-the-eye* would be a *harassment* to the Children of Israel, so would those people be a *harassment* to them if they allowed them to remain in the land.

Is that right?

"Those which ye let remain of them shall be *pricks* in your eyes and *thorns* in your sides."

Paul said, "there was given to me a *thorn* in the *flesh.*" If Paul's *thorn* was sickness, then this *thorn is sickness,* but we can see, right from these words, that he's talking about people.

Joshua was speaking to the people, and he told them that if they didn't do certain things, then this is going to be the result. *"Know for a certainty,* (no doubt about this) *that the Lord your God will no more drive out any of these nations from before you; but they shall be snares and traps unto you, and scourges in your sides, and thorns in your eyes, until ye perish from off this good land which the Lord your God hath given you" (Joshua 23:13).*

"Thorns in your eyes." Now what is he talking about there?

He is talking about *people.* He's talking about the inhabitants of the land, the people who lived in the land, is that right?

All right, that's two witnesses. The Bible says, *"In the mouth of two or three, let every word be established" (Matthew 18:16)*

"But the sons of Belial shall be all of them as thorns thrust away, because they cannot be taken with hands:" (II Samuel 23:6)

David is speaking in the above verse. These sons of Belial represented the children of Satan, those who were opposed to the commandments and the will and purpose of Almighty God. David isn't talking about *disease, or sickness.* He is talking about people.

He says, "the sons of Belial, (what about them?) shall be all of them as thorns, thrust away, because they cannot be taken with hands." So he calls these sons thorns. Can you see it?

In all of these cases the word *thorn* is used metaphorically, as an illustration of what it would be like *in the natural* if you would be stuck in the side with a literal thorn from a rose bush.

All right, let's go back to the 12th chapter of II Corinthians. Keep in mind that the *"thorns"* that we've been reading about were all persons, not diseases or sicknesses, but *persons.*

In the 7th verse, Paul says, *"And lest I should be exalted above measure through the abundance of the revelations, there was given to me a thorn in the flesh."* This verse tells you exactly what the *"thorn" is.* You have to be *deaf, dumb, blind, or dishonest* not to see it.

As you know, the word *messenger* means *angelos* in the Greek: we derive our English *word* angel from it. In the *GREEK NEW TESTAMENT,* in which the *NEW TESTAMENT* was originally written, the word *angelos* is found approximately 188 times. It is translated 181 times as *"angel"* and translated *"messenger"* seven times. In every single one of those 188 times it always refers to a *person* and not a *thing*.

What Paul was saying was that Satan dispatched one of his *demonic angelic spirits* to harass him and make his life miserable. If you read the account of the Apostle Paul, through the book of ACTS, and then through the EPISTLES that he wrote, you'll find that everywhere he went he was persecuted. He was stoned, whipped, shipwrecked, and thrown into prison. Those demons didn't want him to get loose, to preach the WORD OF GOD.

They followed him like a blood-hound and bugged him everywhere he went.

Now, surely God is not in partnership with the devil. He doesn't use the devil as *such,* and send the devil to His own man.

But Paul said, *"There was given to me a messenger of Satan,"* and then we find out what the *messenger of Satan* was sent to do.

"There was given to me a messenger of Satan to buffet me." In the Greek, the word "buffet" means to strike with the hand or hit with the fist, blow after blow after blow after blow. If this was a sickness, Paul would have to have been sick all of his lifetime to fullfill the meaning of the word buffet.

I've heard some people say — and I've had to say it sometimes — "Man — that *guy* is a pain-in-the-neck."

You don't mean that the *guy* is literally wrapped around your neck with a *strangle-lock* on you.

You mean that, just as a pain-in-the-neck would annoy you, that *guy* — every time you see him — gives you a *"pain-in-the-neck!"*

MESSENGER OF SATAN — THORN IN THE SIDE — PAIN IN THE NECK!

When Paul was on his way to the city of Damascus, he was a Pharisee; he *had not yet* met Jesus Christ as his Saviour, and he was breathing out threatenings against the church. He was persecuting the church.

But, Paul met the Lord in a *divine-encounter.* After he had fallen to the ground, and he opened his eyes, he was blind; he went into the city.

God spoke to a man named Ananias. Ananias went and laid hands on Paul. The scales fell off of his eyes, he immediately saw, was filled with the Holy Ghost, and was baptized.

God spoke to Ananias, and told him to go minister to Paul. Then the Lord said, *"For I will show him how great things he must suffer for my name's sake" (Acts 9:16).*

Now, the connotation that immediately comes to your mind when you think of *"suffering"* is sickness, physical pain, or anguish. There are over 15 different Greek words that are translated *"suffer."* I looked them *up* — every one of them — and do you know there is a marvelous revelation that comes out of it? Do you know, that in not one of those 15 cases, is the word *"suffer"* ever applied to a Christian suffering sickness or disease. NOT ONE TIME!

That's why you have to study the Bible to understand and know what the *words* mean.

I wanted to know because I have a responsibility to preach to the people. I don't want to preach *garbage.* I don't want to give you something that's not true. I'd rather not preach at *all,* than to preach something that's erroneous, and false. The Bible says it is a terrible thing to fall into the hands of the living God. Man, you had better not play with God. Some are doing *that.* You may think that you are getting away with *it* because God doesn't drop the *hammer* on you. But let me tell you something. *JUDGMENT DAY* is coming, and you're going to answer to God. Whether you like it or not, you will answer to God.

I don't want that! I don't want it — so I'm going to give you everything I have right now. You can take it or leave it. You can like it or dislike it. You can spit on me and stop going to church. You can throw rocks at me — whatever you want — I've discharged my duty.

When I stand before the Lord, all I plan to hear Him say is, "Well done thou good and faithful servant".

That will be enough for me! "Enter into the joy of thy LORD." That's what I'm looking for! Right?

When I found that not one time does the word *"suffer"* (in those 15 different Greek words) apply to Christians being sick with disease or sickenss, NOT ONCE!, that thrilled my heart!

It confirmed what I already knew — but it just confirmed it along different lines and made me much more bolder to tell the devil, "Get out — I don't plan to take or receive any of your diseases."

If you will read the life of Jesus, in MATTHEW, MARK, LUKE, and JOHN — the four Gospels — you will notice one outstanding fact — *JESUS WAS NEVER SICK!*

The Bible calls Jesus the "Head of the church", and He calls the church *"His Body"*. Now, do you know it's impossible for your head to be sick and not your body? It's impossible for your body to be sick and not affect your head. If Jesus — while He was on the earth — wouldn't tolerate any sickness in *His body,* why does he want to tolerate any sickness in *His body* now that He's seated at the righthand of the Majesty on High?

"Jesus Christ the same yesterday, today and for ever" *(Hebrews 13:8).*

God Himself said, *"I am the Lord and I change not"* (Malachi 3:6). So — whatever He was yesterday — He is today; and whatever He is today — He was yesterday; and whatever He was yesterday — He will be tomorrow; and whatever He is tomorrow — He will be forever!

Nowhere in the Bible does it ever say — in reference to God — "I WAS." God has always been — "I AM." He was "I AM" yesterday, He's "I AM" today, and He'll be "I AM" tomorrow. HE IS "I AM". PRAISE GOD!

If Jesus didn't want sickness in His body then, He doesn't want sickness in *His body now.* That ought to tell you that it's not possible that God could want anybody sick. *NOT IN HIS BODY!*

What is Jesus talking about here when He says, *"I'll show him how great things he must suffer"* (Acts 9:16).

Well, let's look at this Scripture again. *"Therefore I take pleasure in infirmities, in reproaches, in necessities, in persecutions, in distresses for Christ's sake: for when I am weak, then am I strong"* (II Corinthians 12:10). Paul specifies some of these *buffetings* here. But something is very evident here in its absence from that statement. He did not say "in sicknesses or diseases"! When Paul is talking about *weakness* here, he refers to *weakness, in reference to God.* He refers to the fact that — humanly speaking — man is weak, com-

pared to God. He is weak and without God — he's nothing.
That's what Paul means when he says, *"for when I am weak,
then am I strong."* Why? Because I am being strong in the
Lord and in the power of His might. It is not my strength,
but it is the strength of the Lord! We — in our own strength
— physically speaking, are weak. We are infirm, in the sense
that's relative to God. But, WHEN GOD IS IN OUR LIFE,
THEN WE ARE STRONG!

You can't talk about Paul's *weakness* until you talk
about his *strength*. See — *he's strong because he is weak in
the flesh* — in the natural, he's weak — *but his power is the
power of God*, therefore he's strong in the Lord.

It seems very peculiar to me that he wouldn't mention,
"in diseases and in sicknesses." This is *very evidently* left out.

Sickness does not originate *with* or come *from* God.
Sickness is of the devil.

Somebody says, "Ah man, you're just trying to *cop
out*, now. You're just trying to put all the burden on the
poor *'ole' devil*, everybody uses the devil as a *'whipping boy.'*

No, I didn't use him. When I came here, I found that the
devil was already here. I didn't put anything on him; the
Lord did it.

You need to realize where disease, sickness, blindness,
deafness, demonic possession, oppression, and all these things
come from; insanity, nervous conditions and people's hair
falling out, holes in their stomachs, worryng, and all of that.
You need to understand that those things do not come from
the Father. They come from Satan.

You need to know that Satan can't put *them* on you unless you're willing to receive them. What Satan does is give
you a symptom, then you go to talking. "I guess I'm going to
be sick." When you say that you just *"signed for the pack-
age."* It's yours now.

"Thou art snared with the words of thy mouth . . ."
(Proverbs 6:2).

*"For with the heart man believeth . . . and with the
mouth confession is made . . ."* (Romans 10:10).

Your mouth — your confession — means a lot. What you
say with your mouth.

*"For verily I say unto you, That whosoever shall say
unto this mountain, Be thou removed, and be thou cast into*

the sea; and shall not doubt in his heart, but shall believe that those things which he saith shall come to pass; he shall have whatsoever he saith" (Mark 11:23).

WHAT YOU SAY WILL PUT YOU OVER OR UNDER. Look back over your whole life, and you'll find that most of the trouble that *you got in* that was really bad and really messed you *up* was because of your mouth. It was because of something you said, or didn't say. Think about it!

Do you remember, Jesus said that the woman should be loosed because she was a *daughter of Abraham?* We are spiritual children of Abraham — *"And if ye be Christ's, then are ye Abraham's seed, and heirs according to the promise" (Galatians 3:29).* If Jesus wanted the *daughter of Abraham* loosed 1900 years ago, He wants the *daughter of Abraham* loosed today. That makes healing available to everybody who is a Christian! It belongs to you, and God wants you to have it. But you have to receive it *by your own faith.* You have to *exercise faith,* believe God, and receive it, or you can't get it — *EVEN THOUGH HE WANTS YOU TO HAVE IT.*

II Timothy 3:12:

"Yea, and all that will live godly in Christ Jesus shall suffer (what?) *persecution."*

In the above verse we find something about what the *sufferings* are. This word that we will use here — "in a nut shell" — sums *up* what the sufferings were that the Lord was talking about to Paul.

These are the only *sufferings* that you, as a Christian, should go through. *"Yea, and all that will live godly in Christ Jesus will suffer* (suffer what?) *persecution."* It didn't say a thing about *suffer sickness,* or *suffer disease,* did it? *IT SAID SUFFER PERSECUTION.*

Now the devil will make you feel guilty and make you feel like you're supposed to suffer a whole lot of *stuff,* because you see, if you have it too easy, well — *that wouldn't be Christianity.* You're not supposed to *have it too easy.*

That's a lie that the devil has perpetrated against the church, and we've swallowed it hook — line — sinker — fishing-pole — reel — the fisherman and his boots — the whole dumb thing.

Yes, you will be persecuted. Jesus said in the 15th chapter of John's Gospel, and the 20th verse; *". . . The servant is*

*not greater than his Lord. If they have persecuted me, they
will also persecute you; if they have kept my saying, they
will keep yours also.*"

You know that with all the persecution they gave Jesus,
it didn't stop Him from doing what He had to do; praise
God! And neither did it stop Paul.

Everywhere Paul went that *spirit* stirred *up* strife, con-
tention, imprisonment, bonds, whippings, and ship wrecks,
and stonings.

But none of it ever stopped Paul from getting the job
done. Paul came to the end of his life, and they didn't kill
him; they didn't *chop off Paul's head,* until he was ready.

Paul said, "*I've fought a good fight, I've kept the faith,
and I've finished my course.*" (There is nothing else to do.
I'm finished. I'm going home.) *I'm ready to be offered up.*
(He didn't say, I'm ready to be killed.) He said, "I'm ready to
offer myself up." And he submitted to the *chopping-block,*
because it was his will, and his determination. He didn't
have to die that way.

Paul didn't *even* have to be in prison; because God is no
respector of persons. If God let Peter out of jail, He would
have let Paul out of jail. Paul didn't want to be out of jail.
He chose to go that way, just as he chose to live without
being married. That was his choice.

"Well Brother Price, what did it mean when it said that
Paul prayed three times, and God said, 'my grace is
sufficient'?"

Certainly God's grace is sufficient.

Do you know what the "*grace of God*" is?

It is authority to use the *Name of Jesus.*

God is not going to do anything else about the devil
until He binds him and throws him into the *bottomless pit.*
Until then it's the churches' responsibility to do something
about Satan and demons.

"*Behold, I give unto you power to tread on serpents
and scorpions, and over all the power of the enemy: and
nothing shall by any means hurt you*" (Luke 10:19).

"*. . . these signs shall follow them that believe; In my
name shall they cast out devils . . .*" (Mark 16:17).

The Bible says, "*Neither give place to the devil*" *(Ephesians 4:27).* That means if he has a place, I gave it to him.

You'll say, "Oh, you'd better be careful what you say, you don't *know* what might happen."

I do know what will happen! My Father told me what will happen. He said, *"I will take sickness from the midst of thee."* He told me what will happen, and I'm just believing and confessing it, and I'm getting healthier every day!

"But in all things approving ourselves as the ministers of God, in much patience, in afflictions, in necessities, in distresses, in stripes, in imprisonments, in tumults, in labours, in watchings, in fastings; By pureness, by knowledge, by longsuffering, by kindness, by the Holy Ghost, by love unfeigned, By the word of truth, by the power of God, by the armour of righteousness on the right hand and on the left, By honour and dishonour, by evil report and good report: as deceivers, and yet true; As unknown, and yet well known; as dying, and, behold, we live; as chastened, and not killed; As sorrowful, yet alway rejoicing; as poor, yet making many rich; as having nothing, and yet possessing all things" (II Corinthians 6:4-10).

Notice, Paul doesn't mention the fact that he was sick.

Let's read another scripture. *"Are they ministers of Christ? (I speak as a fool.) I am more; in labors more abundant, in stripes above measure, in prisons more frequent, in deaths oft. Of the Jews five times received I forty stripes save one. Thrice was I beaten with rods, once was I stoned, thrice I suffered shipwreck, a night and a day I have been in the deep. In journeyings often, in perils of water, in perils of robbers, in perils by mine own countrymen, in perils by the heathen, in perils in the city, in perils in the wilderness, in perils in the sea, in perils among false brethren; in weariness and painfulness . . ."* (II Corinthians 11:23-27).

The word *weariness*, as it is used in the Greek, is the word *labor*, and the word *painfulness* in the Greek is the word *toil*. Paul is saying, "In labors and toils, in watchings often, in hunger and thirst, in fastings often, in cold and nakedness . . ."

Notice the absence of any mention of him being sick.

Now who but Satan's messenger could have brought all of this harassment on a man?

No! Praise God, the "THORN" was not sickness. It was a messenger of Satan.

When Paul prayed, and God said, "I will not remove it," He meant that He wasn't going to get rid of the devil yet.

THERE IS COMING A DAY; but until then He has given *you GRACE,* and He has given *you AUTHORITY,* and He has given *you POWER,* to do something about the devil.

"Resist the devil and he will flee from you" (James 4:7).

PAUL'S THORN IN THE FLESH WAS A MESSENGER OF SATAN.

3

Seven Scriptural Ways to Healing

Part 1

The Heavenly Father is so desirous of His children walking in divine and perfect health, that He has made at least seven ways — that I know of — available to the Christian, whereby he can receive bodily or physical healing, whereby he can walk in divine health, whereby he can be truly the temple of the Living God.

I believe that it is time that we deal with them — from the standpoint of the Word of God — and very clearly delineate these seven different methods of Scriptural healing.

We will deal with the first three *"Scriptural Ways to Healing"* in this Chapter; then cover the remaining four ways in Chapters IV, V and VI.

In spite of all of our scientific advancements, in spite of our ability to have hurled a man over five hundred thousand miles round trip to the surface of the moon and that man stepping forth from an earth-made vehicle and walking across the plains of the moon, the human race is still decimated with sickness and disease. Even in the ranks of Christians there are vast numbers who are, at this very moment, in bodily pain, misery, and affliction. They do not know, for sure, if it is God's will for them to be healed.

In these seven ways, or methods, you can find certainly at least one way whereby you can receive healing for your physical body.

METHOD NO. 1. ANOINT WITH OIL

"Is any sick among you? let him call for the elders of the church; and let them pray over him, anointing him with oil in the name of the Lord: And the prayer of faith shall save the sick, and the Lord shall raise him up; and if he have committed sins, they shall be forgiven him. Confess your

faults one to another, and pray one for another, that ye may
be healed. The effectual fervent prayer of a righteous man
availeth much" (James 5:14-16).

"*Is any sick among you?*" I would have you note, my
friends, that the Bible says, "*Is any sick among you?*" That
any would include *everybody* who is sick, would it not? It
doesn't leave anybody *out*. It doesn't leave out the Apostle
Paul, it doesn't leave out John, it doesn't leave out you or
me. Praise God! "*Is any*" means *anybody* — man, woman,
boy, girl, black, white, green, yellow, educated, uneducated,
poor, rich, indifferent, whatever you are — the Bible says,
"*Is any sick among you?*"

If so, this is what God tells you to do; this is God's direction to you. Listen to it. "*Is any sick among you? Let him call*
for the elders of the church; and let them pray over him,
anointing him with oil in the name of the Lord: And the
prayer of faith shall save the sick, and the Lord shall raise
him up; and if he have committed sins, they shall be forgiven
him. Confess your faults one to another," — it didn't say confess your sins — "*and pray one for another, that ye may be*
healed." See, we ought to pray for one another — "*that ye*
may be healed." This is a clear directive from the throne of
Heaven. "*The effectual fervent prayer of a righteous man*
availeth much."

"Well," you say, "I'm not very righteous."

You say that because you are ignorant of the WORD OF
GOD. The Word of God says that righteousness is a *gift* and
that Jesus Christ was made *our righteousness*. He was made
righteousness for us. **We** are *in Him* and therefore *we are*
righteous.

Not by WHAT WE DO — but because *WE ARE IN*
CHRIST JESUS — He is our righteousnss. If you are a
Christian, *you are righteous*. That means — if you are right-
eous — you can have an effectual, fervent prayer.

Notice, it says if a man is sick, let him call for the elders
of the church and let them pray over him, *anointing him*
with oil.

Now you don't have to do it this way, but it is *one way*
that you can get your healing. It is *one way that will work*.
This method is primarily for those who are so weak and
feeble *in that they cannot muster up enough faith to pray*

for themselves. They are so decimated with disease and so weak in their faith that they can't even dare to believe that God would hear their prayer and heal them. So God has provided this method whereby that person whose faith is very weak can *call in help* for himself. He can receive the healing power of God into his body, by the elders coming and anointing him with oil.

The reason the oil is used in this method is because the person is so weak in faith that he cannot exercise faith in *that which he cannot see.*

Of course, some know that the Word says, ". . . *faith is the evidence of things not seen*" (Hebrews 11:1). But his faith is so weak that he can't muster it up to believe in anything he can't see. He needs something tangible, something that he can *see,* something he can *touch,* something he can *feel.*

When the oil is applied to his head, he can reach *up* with his finger and touch the oil, he can look down and see it glistening on his fingers, and he can release his faith in that oil.

It is not the oil that heals, but it is the oil that *releases his faith* in the *prayers of the righteous,* and they will avail much.

Even though you are very feeble in your faith, *God wants you healed.* He has provided this method for you to *get healing* (by the anointing with oil). It doesn't mean that you love God any less than the person who has strong faith. It just means that you are still an *infant in faith,* and you haven't arrived at that point of maturity yet. Thank God you don't have to wait until you get mature to get healed. Even though you are *weak* and infantile in your spirit and in the things of faith, God has provided this method. He is primarily healing you — not by anything you do, but by the *prayer of faith* prayed by the people who anointed you with oil.

Let's look at an illustration of this method — the anointing with oil — as it was used in the ministry of the Apostles. When Jesus had sent the Apostles out to minister, He gave them authority, and on certain occasions — they anointed with oil, as a point of contact for the sick person to release his faith in the power of God. "*And they cast out many devils,* (or demons) *and anointed with oil, many that were sick, and healed them" (Mark 6:13).*

So, we see that the anointing with oil is a Scriptural method; it is a God ordained way; but it is not the only way. You don't have to do it this way, but it is available to you. If your faith is weak, praise God, you don't have to languish in the confines of disease and sickness. You don't have to be in pain and misery, spending all of your days in bed and spending all of your money on medicine. You can call for the elders of the church and have them lay their hands on you and *anoint you with oil,* and you can reach *up* and touch that oil and say, "Bless God, I can't bring my faith up to believing on my own, but thank you Father, for I know this is a sign of your willingness to heal me."

Then, God said, "the prayer of faith — not the prayer of doubt, not the prayer of hope, but the prayer of faith — "shall save the sick, and the Lord shall raise him up." That means HE WILL BE HEALED — doesn't it?

Understand again, you do not have to do it this way. It is only one of the seven ways to receive your healing. But it is a Scriptural way, and God will honor it, and you can be healed by this method — *THE ANOINTING WITH OIL.*

METHOD NO. 2. IF TWO OF YOU SHALL AGREE ON EARTH AS TOUCHING ANYTHING

"Again I say unto you, That if two of you shall agree on earth as touching anything that they shall ask, it shall be done for them of my Father which is in heaven. For where two or three are gathered together in my name, there am I in the midst of them" (Matthew 18:19-20).

Most people have taken the above Scriptures as an excuse for having small church services, little congregations, and little insignificant prayer-groups.

They say, "Bless God — we don't have to have a lot of people; the Lord said if just two or three are gathered together, He is in the midst."

Thank God that is true — He is there — if you are by yourself, He is there. But, that is not what the above Scripture is referring to.

Jesus is saying here, *"if two of you shall agree on earth as touching anything,"* (that would have to include healing, or else it's not anything, isn't that right? If it didn't include healing, it would be — *only some things,*) "it shall be done."

He didn't say, might be done. He didn't say there was a 50/50 chance of it. He said *"it shall be done."*

This second method is for people whose faith is operating at perhaps only 50 percent efficiency. If you can get two people with 50 percent faith, you can put them together and you have 100 percent — that's the whole idea.

Literally — in the Greek — Jesus is saying, "Wherever two or three are gathered together, there am I in the midst of them to make that good that they have agreed upon."

He can't make it good if we don't agree.

And Jesus said, *"I AM IN THE MIDST OF THEM TO MAKE THAT GOOD THAT THEY HAVE AGREED UPON."*

YOU MUST AGREE. The method here is *AGREEING*. IF YOU ARE NOT AGREEING, IT WON'T WORK.

That is the reason that many Christians you have prayed for have died.

You wonder — "Why did they die? We were praying for them to be healed."

What you didn't know was that all that time the person was hoping to go on to Glory. You wanted him healed, but he was ready to die. There is no *agreement* there, and God can't answer that prayer.

He said that you would have to agree.

Many times, people don't understand and that is the reason that I am so laborious in explanations. I talk out of experience, and I have had enough dealings with people over twenty years to know that, even though they are sitting there in that pew, with their eyes open, looking at me, many times their mind is somewhere else, and they don't even hear me. I will keep saying it over and over again, line upon line, precept upon precept, here a little, there a little, and then maybe some of you will finally perceive what I am saying.

Sometimes when I pray for people and I tell them, "Look, we will agree, and I will lay my hands on you, and we are going to believe that you receive your healing, according to the Word of God. Is that all right with you?"

"Yes, Yes," they say.

"Will you believe that God heals you now?" I ask.

"Yes, yes."

I lay my hands on them in all confidence and faith and I pray — and I sometimes feel the power of God flowing into their bodies. I know that God has sent His healing power into them.

When I get finished with the prayer, I say, "Well, bless God, do you believe you are healed?"

"I certainly hope so," they reply.

Well — see we didn't agree. I am believing that they are healed, and they are *hoping* so. Can you see? That is not agreement. That won't work.

That is what has happened many times; you talk to people, and you think that they are believing and agreeing with you, and they are hoping that they will get it.

I will never forget, I was never so scared in all of my life as I was when I first entered into this kind of teaching. A lady came to the church. The first time I saw her she looked like "death-walking", she looked like a skeleton with skin stretched over it, she looked like her next step would be her last. That is how weak she looked.

Somebody had told her about the church. Somebody had told her about what God was doing, and she came to the church. She heard the WORD, and when we had the healing service she came *up*. I explained it to her the best that I could.

She said, "Yes Pastor" in a very weak voice.

And in all faith and confidence, I laid my hands on her, and I believed that God healed her at that moment. I believe that the healing power of God was ministered to her.

I said, "Do you believe that you are healed?"

She weakly said, "Yes."

Her kidneys had failed and she was on a *kidney-machine*. She had to go back to the hospital periodically and be *put on this machine*.

A week or so went by, and on a Sunday night she called me on the telephone.

I said, "How are you doing?"

"Fine," she answered — then she said something that almost scared me to death.

"I'm getting ready to go to the hospital to have a *kidney-transplant.*"

Now — I will tell you why it scared me — *I believed* that she had received her healing when I *laid hands* on her. *But* she kept coming back; she sat under the WORD; and she found out how to act on the Word of God. She went to the hospital; she had a successful kidney transplant; and she is healed now.

See — God *can* work through that. But He can work without that, if you let Him!

Later on, I talked to her, and do you know what I discovered? From the very time that she had had the trouble with the kidney, the doctors had encouraged her to have a kidney transplant. They told her that she was the next one on the list. And as soon as a donor was available, they would give her that kidney.

When she stood in the front of that church, and I laid my hands on her and asked her if she would believe she received the healing, all the time in the back of her mind she was expecting to get it by getting a transplant.

We *didn't agree* — and it scared me — I had just launched *out* into this *thing,* and I thought, "Wow, if this woman dies, wow."

SEE — WE DIDN'T AGREE. All the time it was her intention to get a kidney transplant. She believed in something else, not in what I was saying.

That is why sometimes people have died. They were not agreeing.

She received enough of the Word and she was smart enough to learn how to use that Word against Satan. I tell you that was a frightening experience for me, because I knew that we hadn't agreed.

I believed when I laid hands on her that was the end of it, *I wasn't looking for a kidney, but she was.*

That is why we have to explain these things, because sometimes they come *up,* and I am agreeing on one thing, and they are agreeing on something else.

But, this verse says, "*That if two of you agree on earth as touching anything that they shall ask, it shall be done for them of my Father which is in heaven. For where two or three are gathered together in my name, there am I in the midst of them"* (Matthew 18:19-20).

That means that we have to be confessing the very same thing in order for this method to work.

"Well," you say, "healing is not mentioned in that verse."

You're right, but it says, *"AGREE ON EARTH AS TOUCHING ANYTHING!"* That means that nothing is left out, so that would include healing — wouldn't it?

Now let me give you a Biblical example of somebody agreeing. *"And when Jesus departed thence, two blind men followed him, crying, and saying, Thou son of David, have mercy on us. And when he was come into the house, the blind men came to him: and Jesus saith to them, Believe ye that I am able to do this? They said unto him, Yea Lord. Then touched he their eyes, saying According to your faith be it unto you. And their eyes were opened"* (Matthew 9:27-30).

He said "according to your faith — not my power but according to your faith."

THEY AGREED WITH JESUS. He said, "do you believe that I am able to do it?" They AGREED.

If they had said, "No, we don't believe that you can do it," do you think that they would have been healed?

That is the second method. Two or more can agree on anything that they ask. *YOU CAN RECEIVE YOUR HEALING BY GETTING SOMEBODY TO AGREE WITH YOU.* Just be *sure* you find out what they are agreeing to.

Don't come up with this junk about, "Well — have a silent request."

SILENT REQUEST! MAN, No way! You had better specify what you want.

It amazes me — our stupidity and our ignorance with our professed education, and our academic acumen, and yet we can be so stupid.

That would be just like driving up to the gas station and your gas-gauge is on *empty* — you push your button, the window goes down, the man comes up and asks, "What can I do for you?"

You say, "I have a silent request."

How much gas would you get in your tank? You had better tell him what you want, right?

"I HAVE A SILENT REQUEST!" Now we think God is just as big a fool — "I *ain't* going to tell you God, I have a silent request."

You say, "Well, God knows our needs."

Sure He does, and the gas station people know that cars need gas; they have gas in the tank, but they don't know how much gas you need — you only get what you ask for. The very fact that the gas station is in existence is indicative of the fact that they know that automobiles need gasoline. But you have to tell them how much you want. Maybe you are only going to drive around the block and you may not need a full tank today, but if you're taking a long trip you will need a whole tank, but the gas station attendant doesn't know that.

If you are going to get somebody to agree with you, he needs to know what you are talking about.

I don't always want to agree with folk.

I had a lady to tell me, "Pastor, I'm just having so much trouble, these burdens are just *weighting* me down. I don't know how I'm going to make it. I want you to pray that the Lord will take half of these burdens from me. I can carry the other half. But just agree with me that the Lord will take half."

I said, "I won't do it, because it is out of line with the Word of God."

The Bible says, *"Casting all your care upon him; for he careth for you"* (I Peter 5:7).

"SEE, if I prayed that He would take half of them, I would be out of line with the Word. I can't agree with that."

Now if she had come up and said agree with me and she would be agreeing for half, and I would be agreeing for all, it wouldn't work. *TWO OR MORE MUST AGREE AS TOUCHING ANYTHING.*

METHOD NO. 3. LAYING ON OF HANDS

Before we look into the third method in the seven Scriptural ways to receive our healing, let me say this — I'm not opposed to doctors or medicine or medical science. In talking about divine healing, I'm not on a harangue to discredit the doctors or do away with hospitals and nurses.

Praise God for all that man has been able to do to help himself.

I'm just telling you that when you find out how to work the things of God, you won't need a doctor.

There are people who are marriage counselors. I never expect to use one. But I'm not going on a rampage to do away with marriage counselors. There are some folks out there who don't know what I know, and they need marriage counselors. There are some people who are sick and diseased, and they don't know that God has healed them; they had better have a doctor or they will die. Some may not be children of God. Healing doesn't belong to them. Many are dying even with the doctor standing at the side of the bed holding their hand.

If you can learn how God works, you won't need a doctor. I'm not against them — thank God for doctors — but I just know a better way!

"And these signs shall follow them that believe; in my name they shall cast out devils; they shall speak with new tongues; They shall take up serpents; and if they drink any deadly thing, it shall not hurt them; they shall lay hands on the sick, and they shall recover" (Mark 16:17-18).

Jesus said, *"they shall lay lands on the sick and they shall recover"*. The laying on of hands is a method whereby we can receive healing.

There are some things that are done and people think that they are done because it is a church doctrine or a particular denominational tradition. I like to do the things that I do because I can find warrant for them in the Word of God. *Laying on of hands* is one of the fundamental principles of the doctrines of Christ. *The laying on of hands* should be practiced by the church to receive the Holy Ghost, to set people apart unto the Lord, to lay hands on them for healing, yes — and even sometimes to cast out demons.

I know that *shoots down* some teachings that you have been led to believe. But I want to remind you of the account of Jesus dealing with the woman who had the spirit of infirmity for 18 years. Jesus called her to Him and laid hands on her and said, *"Woman thou art loosed from thine in-*

firmity." He laid His hands on her and cast that spirit out of her.

The *laying on of hands* is Scriptural and you can receive your healing that way.

Hebrews 6:1-2:

1 Therefore leaving the principles of the doctrine of Christ, let us go on unto perfection; not laying again the foundation of repentance from dead works, and of faith toward God,

2 Of the doctrine of baptisms, and of laying on of hands, and of resurrection of the dead, and of eternal judgment.

Did you notice in the above Bible verses, it didn't say the principles of the Baptist Church, or the principles of the Lutheran Church, or the Jehovah's Witnesses, or the principles of the Mormons, but the *principles of the doctrine of Christ.*

Jesus Himself, in ministering to the sick, used the laying on of hands more than any other method.

Let's see what Mark's gospel has to say. "*And when Jesus was passed over again by ship unto the other side, much people gathered unto him: and he was nigh unto the sea. And behold, there cometh one of the rulers of the synagogue, Jairus by name; and when he saw him, he fell at his feet, And besought him greatly, saying, My little daughter lieth at the point of death: I pray thee, come and lay thy hands on her, that she may be healed; and she shall live . . .*" (Mark 5:21-23).

It makes a difference when people believe in it. If you don't believe in the *LAYING ON OF HANDS*, it is hard to make it work for you. But if you will believe in it *IT WILL WORK!*

If you read the whole story, you know that it worked for Jairus.

Jesus went in and laid hands on this little girl; she had died by the time Jesus arrived, but He took her by the hand and called her spirit back from the spirit world, and she arose and was made alive!

Jairus believed in the laying on of hands. He said, "*Come and lay hands on my little girl that she may be healed.*"

"And he cometh to Bethsaida: and they bring a blind man unto him, and besought him to touch him. And he took the blind man by the hand, and led him out of the town; and when he had spit on his eyes, and put his hands upon him, he asked him if he saw ought. And he looked up, and said, I see men as trees, walking. After that he put his hands again upon his eyes, and made him look up: and he was restored, and saw every man clearly" (Mark 8:22-25).

In the above Scripture Jesus put His hands on the man twice. It is all right to put your hands on folks twice. Notice this — it didn't say He prayed. It said He put His hands on him.

So — *LAYING ON OF HANDS* is another method that you can use to receive healing. You remember the first method that we talked about. It is found in the Book of James, where they prayed over the sick and anointed them with oil, of course hands would have to be laid on him there, but the oil is involved in that method. In this method you just lay your hands on them as a *point of contact* to release their faith in the healing power of God. *YOU CAN RE-CEIVE HEALING! BY THE LAYING ON OF HANDS!*

". . . And they shall lay hands on the sick and they shall recover" (Mark 16:18) Praise God! I have seen hundreds of people recover when I laid hands on them. Not because it was Fred Price, but because Fred Price dared to believe what Jesus said! I'm a believer — and it belongs to me, so I lay my hands on them and bless God! They get healed!

4

Seven Scriptural Ways to Healing
Part 2

A young woman called me on the telephone one day and said, "Fred, I just want to thank you for your ministry. I want to thank you for giving us the Word of God. I want to thank you for showing us how to *use* God's Word. A friend of mine called me and she was sick, and I was able to tell her what to do. I was able to take the Word of God and show her that healing belonged to her and sickness didn't belong to her. She lives way out east of Los Angeles, and I'm going out and talk with her."

My friend wasn't sick, but she listened to the Word, and she was able to help somebody else.

You may not be physically sick, and God forbid that you should ever be, but sooner or later you will run into someone who is sick. And wouldn't it be a thrill to be able to help them? That is why I want you to see these truths.

METHOD NO. 4. GIFTS OF HEALINGS

"For to one is given by the Spirit the word of wisdom; to another the word of knowledge by the same Spirit; To another faith by the same Spirit; (this is a special faith — not saving faith, but special) *to another gifts of healing by the same Spirit.* (In the Greek it is gifts of healings — plural, not singular). *To another the working of miracles; to another prophecy, to another discerning of spirits, to another divers kinds of tongues; to another the interpretation of tongues: But all these worketh that one and the selfsame Spirit, dividing to every man severally as he will"* (II Corinthians 12:8-11).

What he is saying is that these things operate as the Spirit wills and not as we will.

Keep that in mind.

Now in that same chapter, let's read verse 28, *"And God hath set some in the church, first apostles, secondarily prophets, thirdly teachers, after that miracles, then gifts of healings ..."*.

God has set them in the church, and I dare anybody to take them out.

Some of these people say, "Well, that went out with the early church. We don't have that anymore."

The thing I always like to ask them is, "How do you know? You weren't there. How can you be so bold to say it went out and you weren't even there? You had better be careful what you take out of God's Word."

The Bible says God has set *"gifts of healings"* in the church, and I have no Scripture *anywhere* that I can find that says God has taken them *out*.

That means that *"gifts of healings"* are still in the church.

"GIFTS OF HEALINGS" is the fourth method that we are going to study about whereby we can receive healing.

"Gifts of healings" do not operate at the will of men, but they operate as the SPIRIT wills. These are supernatural manifestations of the "Gifts Of The Spirit". God has set these *gifts* in the church. *Gifts of healings* work as the SPIRIT WILLS.

They work through certain *ministries*. We have a good illustration of the *"gifts of healings"* being manifested in the ministry of Kathryn Kuhlman.

You see, *"gifts of healings"* will heal people whether they are saints or sinners. They are actually and primarily for the unbeliever. It's really to attract attention unto the power of God, that they may know the reality of the POWER OF GOD.

If you've ever been to one of Kathryn Kuhlman's services — you know it works. It attracts sinners, and when people are being healed she puts out the invitation and *spreads the net* — and bless God! All manner of people come and get saved.

Now Kathryn Kuhlman doesn't actually heal anybody, but because she is a New Testament type evangelist, she has *gifts of healings, word of knowledge* and sometimes *working of miracles* in manifestation in her ministry. Consequently, many times people will be healed whether they have faith or not.

The only thing about this method is that you can never be sure that you will be the *one who is healed;* so if the doctor has given you six months to live and told you that you have a terminal case — you have cancer and it's inoperable — well, you can't afford to sit around and blow five of those six months waiting for someone to come to town who has these special manifestations in their ministry, since it is as the *Spirit wills,* and your faith has nothing to do with it, and you don't know whether or not it will be His will for you to be healed *that way.* (*IT IS GOD'S WILL FOR YOU TO BE HEALED.*) But in this *SPECIAL MANIFES-TATION* it is the Holy Spirit that is operating. It is as *THE HOLY SPIRIT WILLS.* You can't initiate this or make it work. It is as the Holy Spirit wills.

If anybody supposedly has *"Gifts of Healings"* and they can turn it off and on when they want to, then something is wrong, because they are doing better than Jesus could do. Even Jesus didn't work *"Gifts of Healings"* as He willed, and I will show you this through the Scripture.

"Now Peter and John went up together into the temple at the hour of prayer, being the ninth hour. And a certain man lame from his mother's womb was carried, whom they laid daily (that would mean every day — wouldn't it?) *at the gate of the temple which is called Beautiful, to ask alms of them that entered into the temple; who seeing Peter and John about to go into the temple asked an alms. And Peter fastening his eyes upon him with John, said, Look on us. And he gave heed unto them expecting to receive something of them. Then Peter said, Silver and gold have I none: but such as I have give I thee: In the name of Jesus Christ of Nazareth rise up and walk. And he took him by the right hand, and lifted him up: and immediately his feet and ankle bones received strength. And he leaping up stood, and walked, and entered with them into the temple, walking and leaping, and praising God"* (Acts 3:1-8).

Now don't you realize that this gate, the gate Beautiful, was a prominent gate leading into the temple? Don't you realize that if this man was laid there daily at the gate it hadn't been too long ago that Jesus passed that way? For three and a half years Jesus taught in the temple. Why had this man never been healed before? I'm sure that Jesus passed that way. We can show accounts where Jesus went into the temple and taught and would have had to enter through the gate Beautiful, because it was one of the prominent gates, yet this man was laid there daily and he didn't get healed.

How come all of a sudden he gets healed?

Because *these* are "gifts of healings".

Remember — this man was not a Christian; he couldn't exercise *Christian faith*.

This was something that the Holy Ghost did on His own. As Peter walked by, suddenly the Spirit of God moved in him and as the lame man asked an alm, Peter was able to say, "In the name of Jesus Christ of Nazareth, rise up and walk."

I am sure Peter had passed that gate before and had passed right by that man and he had never been healed.

You mean to tell me that all of a sudden Peter generated interest in the man? No! But when *"gifts of healings"* are in operation, you have to wait for the Spirit to move.

This is where many have missed it. They have tried to categorically put all healings in the same classification. They will see somebody in a wheel chair and they think that all you have to do is tell them to "Rise and walk in Jesus' name."

Somebody told me that they had gone to a *service* and several people who were in wheel chairs were instantly healed. They got up and started walking.

There was another lady there, and she said, "Bless God, I am going to do the same thing." She attempted to get out of her wheel chair and fell to the floor. They had to put her back into that wheel chair.

"Well," you say, "why?"

Because "gifts of healings" work as the Spirit wills, not as you will.

Many people think that Jesus went around and healed anybody, any time He wanted to, but He didn't. Jesus was a prophet and He ministered as a prophet under the *anointing* of the Spirit of God. There were some things that He could only do when the Spirit of God moved on Him.

If you will read the four Gospels, you will notice all the different and diverse ways that Jesus healed people — not actually Jesus — but God through Him.

Did you ever wonder why He never did the same thing all of the time?

Some of these things work in certain ways and you have to work them the way they are supposed to be worked or they won't work.

In the Book of John 5:1-9, it says this, *"After this there was a feast of the Jews; and Jesus went up to Jerusalem. Now there is at Jerusalem by the sheep market a pool, which is called in the Hebrew tongue Bethesda, having five porches. In these lay a great multitude of impotent folk, of blind, halt, withered, waiting for the moving of the water. For an angel went down at a certain season into the pool, and troubled the water; whosoever then first after the troubling of the water stepped in was made whole of whatsoever disease he had. And a certain man was there, which had an infirmity thirty and eight years. When Jesus saw him lie and knew that he had been now a long time in that case, he saith unto him, Wilt thou be made whole? The impotent man answered him, Sir, I have no man, when the water is troubled, to put me into the pool: but while I am coming, another steppeth down before me. Jesus saith unto him, Rise, take up thy bed, and walk. And immediately the man was made whole, and took up his bed, and walked: and on the same day was the sabbath."*

Well, don't you know that was kind of cruel of Jesus, very thoughtless of Him, very callous and hardhearted of Him? IF JESUS went around and healed everybody, whenever He decided to, it was kind of cruel of Him to only heal this one man. Notice that the Holy Ghost puts in there that there was a *"great multitude of people,"* and He only healed one person.

I'll bet the other people surely were hurt. I'm sure they probably said, "Why not me? I've been here a long time."

But you see, this was *THE GIFTS OF HEALINGS* in operation, and when they are in operation only the one that the Holy Spirit singles out can be healed.

Do you understand? That man was the one who the Holy Spirit directed Jesus to. Nobody else could get healed under those circumstances by that particular manifestation, because it is as the HOLY SPIRIT WILLS.

Not as Jesus wills, but the Spirit.

Sometimes in this kind of healing certain things are required of you by God; that is, in order for these *gifts of healings* to manifest themselves. If you don't do what He says, then you won't receive your healing. Notice, Jesus said, *"Arise, take up your bed"*. All of that was a part of the process, and the man had to be obedient to this.

In this particular account we have the story of the blind man. *"And as Jesus passed by, he saw a man which was blind from his birth. And his disciples asked him saying, Master, who did sin, this man, or his parents, that he was born blind? Jesus answered, Neither hath this man sinned, nor his parents: But that the works of God should be made manifest in him. I must work the works of him that sent me, while it is day: the night cometh, when no man can work. As long as I am in the world, I am the light of the world. When he had thus spoken, he spat on the ground and made clay of the spittle and he anointed the eyes of the blind man with the clay, and said unto him, Go, wash in the pool of Siloam (which is by interpretation, sent). He went his way, therefore, and washed, and came seeing"* (John 9:1-7).

Well, let me ask you this, If he had not gone and washed, do you think he would have been healed?

No!

You say, "Why did Jesus spit on the ground, and put that unsanitary stuff on his eyes, and tell him to go, and wash it off?"

I don't know — ask Jesus! I'm sure that blind man could have cared less if he had put *cow-manure* on his eyes; he received his healing, didn't he?

Why did Jesus do it that way?

I don't know. I don't have all the answers.

Do you know anybody who does? Because if you do know anybody who has all the answers, I want you — when you find him — to hold him in that position, and I want to make a great big sign, about 20 by 30 feet, and I want to put this sign over him, while I take his photograph, and on the sign I'm going to write — "THE BIGGEST LIAR I HAVE EVER KNOWN!"

No, no one has all of the answers.

I tell you, I don't believe that blind man cared. He received his sight. He had never seen a day in his life, and bless God he received his sight!

But he would not have been healed if he had not obeyed Jesus. He had to go to the pool of Siloam and wash it off. Sometimes the Lord will have us do these things to release our faith. I don't know *why* He does it like that, but He does.

When we are obedient to it, we receive the benefits and that is what counts, isn't it?

In II Kings 5:9-14 is the account of the Assyrian soldier named Naaman who had leprosy. I will paraphrase. Naaman heard that there was a prophet of God over in the land of Israel, and he went over there, and the prophet Elisha didn't even come out and talk to Naaman. Naaman was a great man — a four star General — maybe even an eight star General! Anyway, he was the biggest man in Assyria. He was the most important military man in the whole country of Assyria, and he came to this prophet's house and the prophet *didn't even come out and talk to him.*

Elisha sent his servant *out* and said, "I'll tell you what to do. You go down to the river Jordan and dip seven times and your flesh will come *clean* — even as a little child."

Well the *upshot* of the story was that Naaman got all *huffy* about it — like some of you do when God tells you to believe that you have received something, and you just want Him to pour it out on you, without exercising faith.

Naaman got *all mad* and *bent out of shape,* and was ready to get into his chariot and go back to Assyria.

But, thank God, he had a servant with him who had some sense — more sense than Naaman did.

The servant said, "Master, if he had told you to do some great exploit, you would have done it. You have come all this way, and you don't have anything to lose, and you need a bath anyway, so why don't you *go on down,* and dip in Jordan?"

So Naamn went down and dipped seven times and his flesh came again as a little child's.

I ask, why did God tell him to dip seven times, why not two times, why not one time? I don't know, but it worked!

In all cases ours is not to know, ours is only to do what the Word of God tells us to do. We ask too many questions. WHY? WHY? WHY?

Just because HE SAID IT! That's why. Do it and you will get results.

We have just looked at two examples — one in the Old Testament and one in the New Testament.

Here is the situation — Jesus spit on the ground and made clay for one man, and put it on his eyes; he washed it off and he received his sight.

In the other He told Naaman to dip seven times in the river Jordan; he did and his flesh came clean.

That was *"GIFTS OF HEALINGS."*

You can't tell every blind man to go down to the pool of Siloam; you can only do it if the Spirit of God tells you to do that.

Kenneth Hagin told this story of how *"gifts of healings"* operated in his ministry on one occasion.

He was in a certain church and preached a message (He ministers with a tangible anointing of God's healing power).

He was getting ready to *minister* to the congregation and suddenly the Spirit of God spoke to him. (Many times you will read in the Old Testament, that the prophets said, "And the Word of the Lord came unto me saying —when you say *hear,* it is not audible so that anyone else around you could hear, but to you it is audible. God spoke to me one time and it was as real to me as if somebody was talking out loud.) And the Spirit of God said to Hagin, "Minister first to people who have something wrong with them from the waist down." He told the congregation what the Lord said and told them to *come up* first and he would minister to them.

Hagin admitted that while these people were coming *up,* he didn't know what he was going to do next.

Well, the *upshot* of the story was that 12 people came forward.

Hagin was trying to reason in his mind, "What am I supposed to do now?"

Then the Spirit of God spoke to him and said, "Tell them to run and everyone who runs will be healed."

Well that isn't too much different than going down to the Jordan and dipping seven times, is it?

He said that there was one man who had been injured on his job; some gasoline had exploded and it *blew up* on his legs and it burned all of the muscles and ligaments. He couldn't bend his legs or extend them. He couldn't lift them off the floor and he had to scoot along.

Kenneth Hagin wondered, "What am I going to tell this man?" Then he looked at him and asked, "Brother, can you run?"

It so startled the man that he said, "My God, No — Run? — I can hardly walk. Didn't you see me come down here?"

Hagin said, "Brother, I am not doing the healing, the Lord told me to tell you that if you would run, you would be healed."

Kenneth Hagin said he never in his life saw a man move so fast. He said that man didn't argue with him, he didn't say anything, he whirled around and scooted down the aisle, and around the church, and Hagin could see that he wasn't any better.

So Hagin wondered, "What am I going to do now? I *know* the Lord spoke to me and told me to tell him to run."

When the man came to the front Hagin said, "Well, do it again."

And as fast as the man could go he went around the church, up the aisle again, and he wasn't any better. He was still scooting.

Again, Hagin wondered, "What am I going to do now?"

There was a little alter rail — Hagin was standing behind it — and suddenly the Spirit of God moved on him, and he jumped over that alter rail and caught that man under the arm and ran down one aisle, around the church, and Bless God! when they came back down the aisle, the man had straightened up and he was just a running!

You say "Why did God do it that way?"

I DON'T KNOW! And I'll wager that man could care less, he was healed!

Now listen, there were 12 people; 11 of those people, as they ran, were healed.

The last one was a woman. Hagin came to her and said, "Sister, can you run?"

And she said, "NO! NO! I can't run."

Hagin said, "I'm not doing the healing, it is the Lord who is healing, and I can only tell you what the Lord told me to tell you."

She said, "Yeah, but I know I can't run."

Hagin said, "These other 11 couldn't run, but they did and they were healed."

She said, "Yeah, but I *know* I can't run."

And she went away. She wasn't healed, even though it was God's will for her to be healed.

She didn't receive healing because she wasn't obedient.

I don't know why God works that way. I could care less, but the thing that I am glad about is that He tells me how He works it so I can get in on it.

What would be tragic is if He did it like this and would not tell us about it. Then we would not have a ghost of a chance, would we?

But, praise God, He tells us and we can *act* on that Word!

That is *"Gifts of Healings,"* and sometimes they operate like that. Sometimes you go wash in the pool of Siloam, sometimes you dip in the river Jordan 7 times, sometimes you run, but whatever God tells you to do, you had better do it.

He may not choose to heal you by this method. That doesn't mean that it is not God's will for you to be healed. It just means that the Holy Ghost is not going to heal you by this method. "Gifts of Healings" won't work for everybody. We don't control the manifestation of that particular gift of the Spirit. But, Thank God, we don't have to wait for "Gifts of Healings" to get healed.

It does work. It attracts attention unto God. It attracts attention unto His power — people know that He is real and that His power is real.

Don't do as *you will,* do as the *SPIRIT WILLS.*

Praise God! *"Gifts of Healings"* is the fourth method in the *SEVEN SCRIPTURAL WAYS TO HEALING.*

5

Seven Scriptural Ways to Healing

Part 3

In the Scriptures there is a particular school of thought called 'Scriptural numerics'. What it means is — in going through the Bible you find certain numbers that are used over and over again. There is a certain Scriptural emphasis placed upon these numbers. For instance, the number *six* is the number of man; it is one short of number *seven*. Seven in the Scriptures is the number of God, or perfectness, or completeness. In the Book of Revelation, the Seven Spirits of God doesn't mean that there are seven different spirits; but the number *seven* is the complete number — the full number. There are seven days in a week; that is a complete week. Six is one short of seven; six is the number ascribed to man, thus the Beast or the False Prophet is 666, not 777.

Well, we don't want to get into that *per se*, however, Seven Scriptural ways to receive healing would be in divine order, wouldn't they? Since the number *seven* is the number of completeness or perfection, therefore there are seven ways to be healed. Praise the Lord!

METHOD NO. 5. SPECIAL ANOINTINGS

We read in Acts 19:11-12, *"And God wrought special miracles By the hands of* (WHO?) *Paul: so that from his* (WHAT?) *body were brought unto the sick handkerchiefs or aprons, and the diseases departed from them, and the evil spirits went out of them."*

Now notice that it says that God wrought special miracles.

It didn't say that God wrought miracles, did it?

It said He did something special, over and above ordinary miracles. That is mind-blowing enough, miracles in themselves — but here, God is talking about some *special miracles.*

It says that He wrought these special miracles by the hands of Paul.

It didn't say that Paul wrought special miracles by the hand of God, it said that God did something by man's hands. God wrought *special miracles* by the hands of Paul.

Notice it didn't say that He wrought *special miracles* by his feet, it didn't say that God wrought them by his ears, but it *says, "God wrought special miracles by His* (Paul's) *hands, so that from his body* (your hands are a part of your body) *there were brought unto the sick, handkerchiefs or aprons and the diseases departed from them and the evil spirits went out of them."*

It wasn't the handkerchiefs or the aprons that did the healing.

Paul would lay hands on these handkerchiefs and aprons and the handkerchiefs and aprons would act as storage batteries, they would receive this power and when they were placed on the bodies of the sick, the power stored up in the handkerchief (just as electricity is stored up in a battery) would be released into their bodies. It would be as though Paul were physically present with them and laid his hands on them. The handkerchief became the channel through which God wrought this *special miracle.*

Notice it says SPECIAL MIRACLES — everybody then wouldn't have this gift. If it says SPECIAL MIRACLES, that wouldn't mean ordinary. If it said ordinary, then perhaps everybody would have it, but this says God wrought Special Miracles — not just miracles.

He didn't say He wrought them by the hands of the church, but He did this through one man — Paul.

I guess God has the prerogative to do that if He so chooses.

In other words, He anointed Paul with a special anointing; it wasn't an ordinary anointing; but something special. He could lay hands on the sick and this power would transfer from his hands into the bodies of the sick — or even into handkerchiefs or aprons — and sometimes they would be placed on the sick and it would drive out the evil spirits and cause healing.

Now we are talking about the fifth way that God has made available by the Scriptures for us to receive healing — by the special way that He uses men's hands.

In Acts 10:38, we find the Apostle Peter preaching at a Gentile's home (named Cornelius). In the process of that ministry, Peter gave forth the definition of the *ministry of Jesus*. He sums up the healing ministry in this 38th verse; in *one verse*, Peter sums up the *whole ministry of Jesus*. *"How God anointed Jesus of Nazareth* (isn't it interesting in the 19th Chapter we read 'And God wrought') *How God anointed Jesus of Nazareth with the Holy Ghost and* (and means something else is coming up — AND) *with power."*

Well, He is power, and He manifests Himself through the nine gifts and manifestations of the Spirit, but there is also something else which God can do if He wants to do it and that is *to anoint men with a special kind of anointing.* Paul had it (how God wrought *special miracles* by the hands of Paul). So God does use some men's hands. He uses *certain men's hands.*

The Bible says that God is always the same — He doesn't change. If He used men's hands back there in the early church, He will have to use the hands of men today.

If He doesn't do this, then He has changed.

"How God anointed Jesus of Nazareth with the Holy Ghost — and with power: who went about doing good, and healing all that were oppressed of the devil; for God was with him."

Everybody won't have this gift. Everybody doesn't need to have it, *but everybody God wants to have it — will have it.* As He wills it, they will have it.

I thank God that He is the same yesterday, today, and forever. I thank God that what He did yesterday, He will do today, and what He will do today, He will do tomorrow, and I thank God that I can count on it. I know I can count on it!

I hope you can count on it.

I thank God that I can — and He is ever the same. He doesn't turn on me, like people do.

The thing that I like most about God is that He knows our hearts and He looks at the heart. He doesn't look at the outside.

We are so quick to judge from outward appearances. We're just ready to find fault and jump on somebody.

But God looks at the heart.

I thank God that He knows my heart.

I am just waiting upon Him, that He will do today what He did yesterday. I know it is so, because HIS WORD IS TRUE.

Keep in mind that we read in Acts 19:11 where "God wrought special miracles by the hands of Paul," and also, "How God anointed Jesus of Nazareth with the Holy Ghost and with power," while we read this very interesting account of how this *Special Anointing* worked in the ministry of Jesus. *"And a certain woman, which had an issue of blood twelve years, And had suffered many things of many physicians, and had spent all that she had, and was nothing bettered, but rather grew worse* (How tragic). *When she had heard of Jesus, came in the press behind, and touched his garment.* (Why would she do such a dumb thing as that?) *For she said, If I may touch but his clothes, I shall be whole. And straightway* (immediately) *the fountain of her blood was dried up;* (apparently she was hemorrhaging) *and she felt in her body that she was healed of that plague. And Jesus, immediately knowing in himself that virtue* (virtue in the Greek, means power) *had gone out of him* (Now that power is the same power that Jesus was anointed with, that Peter was talking about when he said 'how God anointed Jesus of Nazareth with the Holy Ghost and with power . . .' — this is that power) *turned him about in the press and said, Who touched my clothes?"* · How did He know somebody touched Him? The woman didn't touch Him, she only touched His clothes. It didn't say she touched His body; He would have known that somebody touched His body; He would have felt the touch. It said, *"she touched his clothes and power went out of him. And his disciples said unto him, Thou seest the multitude thronging thee and sayest thou, Who touched me? And he looked round about to see her that had done this thing. But the woman fearing and trembling, knowing what was done in her, came and fell down before him and told him all the truth. And he said unto her, Daughter, thy faith hath made thee whole; go in peace and be whole of thy plague"* (Mark 5:25-34).

Now isn't it interesting that the Bible said that *power* went out of Him, but Jesus *didn't say that the power healed her?*

On God's side — the power went out of Him — but on man's side — it wasn't the power that did it. IT WAS HER FAITH that ignited that POWER — just like you can have gasoline in a can, and it can be a potential bomb, but you have to light a match to it before it will explode. It is really the match that makes it explode.

HER FAITH WAS THE MATCH THAT MADE THAT POWER EXPLODE IN HER BODY.

Jesus didn't say God made you whole; He didn't say the Holy Ghost made you whole; He didn't say the power made you whole; He said *"DAUGHTER YOUR FAITH MADE THEE WHOLE."* Hallelujah! That faith caused that power to flow out.

We want that power to flow out, but we must put the match to it; we have to *light the fuse.*

We want God to light the fuse.

No, God has provided the explosive; we have to provide the fuse. The *fuse* is FAITH.

He said to her, *"Your faith did this."* But you see, Jesus was anointed with that power and it flowed out of Him. He didn't even lay hands on her. He was so saturated with that power that His clothes were filled with it.

Now I can understand that very easily. I fly a lot, traveling from one place to the other. When you get in that *box,* there are not too many places you can go. You can't climb out of the window and go where you want to go, so you are *kind of hemmed in!*

Even though they have a *No Smoking Section,* the smoke doesn't have too many places to go, so it finally drifts down to the section where you are. And, do you know? I have gotten off of that airplane, gone from the airport to my home, gone into the bedroom, took off my coat, and got ready to hang it up in the closet, and it smelled just like cigarettes.

I haven't been smoking, but my clothes smelled just like cigarettes because I was in that environment.

You see, Jesus was *anointed with that power* and it was *in His body.* By *osmosis* as it were, it filtered *out of His body, into His clothes,* and all she did was *touch His clothes.* Glory to God!

In MATTHEW, Chaper 14 you will see something else about the fifth Scriptural way to receive your healing — *Special Manifestations.* I like to call it *SPECIAL ANOINT-INGS.*

As I pointed out before, everybody doesn't have this; everybody won't have it; and it is not necessary that everybody has it. But that person whom God anoints will have it and will be able to use it as the Spirit wills.

Here is an example in the 34th through the 36th verses. *"And when they were gone over, they came unto the land of Gennesaret. And when the men of that place had knowledge of him, they sent out into all the country round about, and brought unto him all that were diseased. And besought him that they might only touch the hem of his garment: and as many as touched were made perfectly whole."*

They touched Jesus by faith; they didn't touch Him out of curiosity; they came believing that if they touched, they would be whole, and they were.

Some people don't believe anything until after God does it.

That is why they never get it. Even though they believe in it. They wonder why it never manifests itself in their lives. They believe it, and what they believe is true, but they *never do anything about what they believe.*

They want God to manifest it first and then they will believe it, and that is not faith. It doesn't work that way.

People who consider themselves intellectually bright really have a problem with this. I am not trying to be funny; they really do have a problem. They know everything with their head.

Faith is not of the head, *faith is of your heart* — *or your spirit.*

Your head just gets in the way — like a roadblock. You have to set your head aside, and this is hard for some people to do, because they feel like, "If I do that, then I'm lowering my standards."

But you are not, you are really being smart for the first time in your life.

The Bible says that God wrought *Special Miracles* by the hands of Paul. The Bible says that God anointed Jesus with the Holy Ghost and with power, in other words, something else besides the Holy Ghost.

Every Spirit-filled believer has the Holy Ghost in him, but every Spirit-filled believer doesn't have this SPECIAL POWER.

Some people like to think that they have this *Special Power*, and they try to *go around* and work *stuff*, and that is why we sometimes mess up.

You had better know what you are anointed with.

Don't try to make something work just because you want it to.

I would love to do it myself in the natural; I would love to press a button and make it work — 24 hours a day — but I can't.

But thank God, I don't have to have that *special anointing* to get the things that I need.

I can use my faith and do that.

Thank God for these special anointings! It attracts attention unto the power of God and lets people know that HIS POWER IS REAL!

Mark 3:10 says, *"For he had healed many; insomuch that they pressed upon him for to touch him, as many as had plagues."*

They wanted to touch Him because they found out that He had this power, and as many as touched Him were healed.

It didn't say that they wanted to touch Peter, James, and John. It said that they wanted to *touch Jesus.*

Everybody wasn't anointed with that power and everyone today is not anointed with that power.

But some are! Thank God for it.

Luke 6:17 says this, *"And he came down with them and stood in the plain and the company of his disciples, and a great multitude of people out of all Judaea and Jerusalem, and from the sea coast of Tyre and Sidon, which came to hear him, and to be healed of their diseases."*

A whole lot of folks want to get healed but they don't want to hear too much; "Just give me a freebie and I will be on my way."

But these people came to *hear.*

Someone called me on the telephone one time — bless her darling heart — Oh, I thank God that He knows my heart, because sometimes in the natural it may look cold-blooded. But, in trying to help people, you don't always help them by trying to *butter them up* and by giving them sweet-milk. You have to give them some green vegetables and they don't always taste good to them.

This woman called and wanted prayer. She said she had heard my radio broadcasts.

Well, I just don't pray for folks just because they *call up.*

Many people think that prayer is a magic wand. But prayer won't work if you're not believing right and acting right.

I started to question her like I usually do.

I asked, "Why did you call?"

"Well, I heard your broadcast, and I want you to pray for this condition in my eyes."

The first thing I asked was, "Have you ever been prayed for before, for this particular condition?"

See, I believe my Father hears prayers and answers prayers. If someone else had prayed for her, and I pray for her again, then I am saying that My Father didn't hear the first person that prayed. I am not knowingly going to do this.

She said, "Yes, they prayed for me out at *Angeles Temple* for this condition."

I was *trying* to help the lady and I asked her, "Why didn't God heal you?"

She said, "Well, if you don't want to pray for me, then I guess I will have to *hang up.*"

I said, "No sister, I want to help you; I'm trying to locate you, I want to find out where you are faith-wise."

"Well, if you don't want to pray, I'll just hang up."

"CLICK!"

"Well," you say, "Why didn't you just pray for her?"

I *believe* that people have to be helped. I don't want them to *get something for now* and *lose it next week* because they don't know how to *stand in faith.* I'm not doing the healing, *God is.* If you get anything from God, you have to *get it by faith.* And if you keep it, you will have to *keep it by faith.* If you don't know how to keep it, the devil is going to steal it — and I don't want him to steal it from you.

Bless God, when I pray I want my prayers to go right from earth to the throne; I expect Him to do something.

I was trying to help her so that she could know how to stand.

So many people don't want help, they just want something for nothing.

These people that we read about in Luke 6 came to *hear* and they wanted to be healed.

I appreciate people who want to hear. Some folks sit and sleep through the service until we get to the healing part, then they are wide awake.

"I know all of that, I don't want to hear!"

Yet they are the ones who are sick. They are the ones sick and messed up — they don't know *squat-doodly*.

If you are not doing it, friend, you don't *know it*, not in the heart. You may know it in the head.

When you know it in the heart and you start doing it, it starts working for you. It works for you then!

All right — *"They came to hear him and to be healed of their diseases."* Praise God. *"and the whole multitude sought to touch him."* It says in verses 18 and 19, *"And they that were vexed with unclean spirits: and they were healed. And the whole multitude sought to touch him: for there went virtue out of him, and healed them all."*

Remember, Peter said, *"How God anointed Jesus of Nazareth with the Holy Ghost and with power: and they touched Him and power went out of Him.*

"Does God heal that way today?"

Sure He does.

I wish that He would heal through me that way. I would like to have that operating in me, but it doesn't and I know it doesn't.

I know that faith works and some other things work, but I don't have this *special anointing*.

Thank God some people do. Kenneth Hagin and Oral Roberts have this *special anointing*.

Oral Roberts has the *anointing* in his right hand, and Kenneth Hagin has the *anointing* in both of his hands.

God anointed Kenneth Hagin in a vision, took him to heaven and touched his palms with His fingers. Hagin said, "Immediately both of my hands began to burn."

That *special anointing* was there and Jesus said He had called him and was giving him a *special anointing* to minister to the sick.

Jesus said, "Go and lay your hands on folks and you will feel that anointing flowing out of your hands into the bodies of the sick." And the beautiful thing about it is, Jesus said, "When you feel that power flow out of your hands into the bodies of the sick, *you will know that they are healed.*"

Now whether or not that manifestation ever happens is up to the people. They have to believe that the man is anointed, and they have to — by faith — receive the anointing or it won't work for them. We want everything to work by itself, we don't want to do anything to help it out. If you don't release your faith, even though a man has a *special anointing,* you won't get healed.

That is why many people in the early days of Oral Roberts ministry called him a "quack." They called him everything but a child of God. They lied about him and accused him because people didn't get healed.

What they didn't understand was, Oral Roberts wasn't healing them and never did claim to heal them.

It was the "anointing" that did it, but you have to *believe* the *man is anointed,* and *receive by faith* — *that anointing.*

This is what people don't understand.

Kenneth Hagin tells this acount about a woman. He had finished his sermon and he was getting ready to minister to the sick. This woman was in the healing line, and she had a little girl who was about 11 years old. She was holding this child in her arms. The child had had polio as an infant, and the child had a brace on her body, from her waist all the way down her right leg to the ankle.

When she came up to be ministered to he asked her, "Do you ever take the brace off?"

The mother said she did only when she bathed the child, other than that she wore it, sleeping or awake. She said if she took the brace off the foot and leg went out to the side and turned over. There was no control over it at all. She told him that in a couple of weeks the doctors wanted to go in and fuse the bones in the ankle, so that the bone would be straight. The child would never be able to move the foot, but at least the foot would be straight.

The mother said, "This is our only child."

The doctors told her when the child reached 16 years of age they would then go into her hip and fuse the bone in her hip, and that would make the leg stiff, and that would be the best that they could do. She would not be able to bend and move that leg. It would always be stiff.

Kenneth Hagin explained to the mother how Jesus had anointed him and what He had told him. He told the mother that all he could do was lay his hands on the child, and for the mother to believe that Hagin was anointed. (She could believe for healing for the child.) So Kenneth Hagin laid his hands on the little girl's leg, and said, "If it will help your faith any, I want you to know that with this child I have a stronger anointing of God's healing power than I have had with anybody that I have ministered to today. I just want to leave my hand there and let it saturate her leg."

He left his hand there and he said that the power went into that leg and into that child.

When he had finished, the mother took the child away. She didn't take the braces off.

See, it is not the minister's prerogative, unless God speaks to him, and definitely tells him, he doesn't *just* go around telling folks to get rid of their wheel chairs, or throw their medicine away.

He doesn't do that because he doesn't know where the individual's faith is.

Now if *you were* doing the healing, then you could say, "throw your glasses away, get rid of your insulin." You are not doing the healing.

My place is to *minister,* and *according to your faith* be it done unto you.

So Hagin said He didn't tell her to take the brace off; it was not his place to do that. If the Lord had spoken to him and said, "Tell that girl to rise up and walk," then he could act on that.

But unless you get that *Word from the Lord,* you are walking on treacherous ground. A whole lot of folks have tried to do that and have fallen flat on their face. Then they give up the whole idea and figure that the entire thing is a fake and a phony. People with good intentions, desiring to see the power of God work, want to help God *out* — "Rise, Brother, Rise in the Name of Jesus — and there is no faith there — and the guy falls flat on his face. It doesn't work because you say it; there has to be some faith involved.

So when the woman reached home it was late, and she put the child to bed.

In the morning she got up, (this is her story afterwards) fixed her husband's breakfast, got him off to work, went in and drew the water for the child's bath — as usual. She went in and woke the child up, brought her into the bathroom, took off her clothes, took the brace off, put her down into the water, and that leg just rose right up into the air, and that ankle just twisted over.

The mother got down on her knees beside the bathtub and began to bathe the child and began to cry and say, "Oh God — I was so in hopes that you would have healed my child last night. I don't want her to have to have this operation. This is my only child — I was so in hopes that you would have healed my child last night. I just knew when Brother Hagin prayed that you would heal her, but she is not healed."

She was looking at that leg, see?

Then her own testimony was, "Suddenly on the inside, something said something (what it really was, was *somebody* — the Greater One was in there — she was Spirit-filled. "Greater is He that is in you than he that is in the world").

The Holy Ghost on the inside said to her, "Do you believe that Brother Hagin lied last night when he said that he was *anointed* with that power? Do you believe that he lied when he said that he felt that *anointing* stronger than he did with anyone else he had ministered to? Do you believe that he both sat and stood there and lied in front of that congregation and said he felt that power?" (Hagin stood a while and then sat as he ministered.)

The woman caught herself, and she began to wipe her tears and she said, "No — No — NO, I don't believe that he lied. *I believe* that Brother Hagin is a *true prophet of God, I believe* that he has the *anointing. I believe* that Jesus appeared to him in that vision, just like he said. *I believe that when he laid his hands on my child, that — that power went out of his hands into her body, and I believe that — that power is in that leg now, working and healing and making that leg every bit whole."*

The woman giving her testimony said that while she was standing there looking in the bathtub at that leg dangling and hanging out in mid-air, she heard something go — "Crack," like you would break some dry sticks, and right before her eyes she saw that leg straighten out — right there in the bathtub the ankle straightened out.

The girl had had *polio* and one leg was smaller in diameter than the other, and instantly the smaller leg became the size of the other! Right while she was standing there looking at it!

The next evening they brought the girl to church and she ran up and down the aisle and ran across the stage demonstrating and showing how she had been healed!

But now — wait a minute — hold it!

God had already healed the girl the night before. That power was in there all the time. But see, *FAITH HAD TO BE RELEASED;* Somebody had to *LIGHT THE FUSE!* before the thing would go off.

The power was in her body, (lying dormant) waiting to explode into healing, and the minute the woman uttered with her mouth — "I believe it" — that is when it happened.

Can't you see how important it is to understand the principles of faith and understand how to cooperate with God?

He wants you healed, but He operates through faith.

We are faith children, of a faith God, and faith must be released by words, through your mouth in order for it to work for you personally.

Can you understand that?

Let me say it again, FAITH, in order for it to work for you personally, has to be released BY WORDS THROUGH your MOUTH.

When the woman said, "I believe, I believe," the power that was already there exploded. The gasoline exploded — her faith was the fuse.

A lot of people have been ministered to and they are still sitting there, like that bomb, ready to go off, but they won't light the fuse. They are going to believe that they are healed after everything passes away.

No, you have to believe it before any manifestation occurs — and *THEN IT OCCURS!* Hallelujah!

There is a story about Smith Wigglesworth, an old time English preacher, who ministered in the last part of the 1800's and the first part of the 1900's. He was a man who lived to be 87 years old and died without sickness or disease. Totally uneducated, he couldn't read anything except the Bible, he couldn't even write his own name until he married — and his wife taught him.

But God used that man to minister on every continent of the world. He went around the world several times. Thousand upon thousands of people were healed in his ministry. Three people were raised from the dead, and he had this *special anointing.*

There was a lady here in the United States who went to the doctor for a routine examination, and the doctors found out that she had cancer, and since they couldn't do anything for her they sent her home to die, saying, "There is no hope; there is nothing we can do."

She had heard that Brother Wigglesworth had been in the United States, but it was too late. He had gone back home to England, across the ocean.

They didn't have airmail like we have now. She was staying in the home of her sister and her husband, so she had her sister to get a handkerchief (remember the 19th chapter of Acts? *"How God wrought special miracles by the hands of Paul so that from his body were brought handker-*

chiefs and aprons . . .") So she had her sister find out Wigglesworth's address and they sent the handkerchief to him — through the mail.

Weeks later, the letter arrived — from England — with the handkerchief in it.

The sister opened the letter, ran into the bedroom where her sick sister was, and said excitedly, "The letter has come from Brother Wigglesworth — the handkerchief is here!"

She read the letter and he told her what to do.

He said for her to gather all the believers who were in the house together — go into the bedroom, join hands, and begin to praise the Lord, and thank Him for the healing, and the power that he (Wigglesworth) was anointed with. He had laid hands on that handkerchief, and he said, "That handkerchief is a storage battery. Now, you lay this handkerchief on her, and her faith will release that power, and the power will explode in her body, and she will be healed."

The sister was so weak, and she was in the bed. The other sister took the handkerchief and laid it on the pillow by her head as she ran out of the house into the back yard, where her husband was working on a car.

She told him that the letter had come and that the handkerchief was there. He had oil all over his hands, and was cleaning up to go into the house, and suddenly they heard all of this commotion. They didn't know *what in the world* was going on. They ran through the hallway into the bedroom, and there was that sister, up out of the bed, just dancing and praising the Lord! doing her thing!

They couldn't understand and said, "What happened?"

This is the account that the sister gave, "As soon as you laid that handkerchief down on that pillow and you walked out of that room, I felt something like a warm glow come out of that handkerchief; it went into the side of my head; I felt it all in my head, then it went down through my body, through my shoulders, into my hands, down my body, into my legs, and it went out through my toes, and when it did, I was healed, and I didn't have a pain — not a symptom —

and I jumped out of the bed and began to praise the Lord."

Glory Hallelujah! Praise God!

Yes, this is a true story.

This is it, the 5th way to receive your healing — "How God wrought *special miracles* by the hands of Paul so that from his body were brought aprons and handkerchiefs and placed on the bodies of the sick." SPECIAL MIRACLES — SPECIAL ANOINTINGS!

You say, "Aw-w-w, I'm not going to believe that."

REMAIN SICK THEN! It won't work for you — anyhow. In fact, it is not even for you. It is only for them who believe. HALLELUJAH!

6

Seven Scriptural Ways to Healing Part 4

As you know, we have been studying the *SEVEN SCRIPTURAL WAYS TO RECEIVE HEALING*.

We have discussed the first five methods, and we are now ready to study the last two methods to receive physical or bodily healing.

METHOD NO. 6. JUST SAYING IT

All right — let's go on to the sixth method. Hallelujah! *"Jesus Christ — the same yesterday, today and for ever"* (Hebrews 13:8).

He never changes; He *NEVER CHANGES;* His Word is ever the same.

You can count on it in the midnight hour — You can count on it when the sun is shining — You can count on it when the rain is falling — and when the floods are rising. HIS WORD IS EVER THE SAME!

I thank God that it is!

You may change; men may change; seasons may change; but the *WORD OF GOD ABIDES FOREVER!* It will accomplish that for which it is sent.

Mark 11:23 says, *"For verily I say unto you, That whosoever shall say unto this mountain, Be thou removed, and be thou cast into the sea; and shall not doubt in his heart, but shall believe that those things which he saith shall come to pass; he shall have whatsoever he saith."*

You say, "Yeah, but He didn't mean a *literal mountain."*

That's what you say — and that's why none of them have ever moved for you. You've limited God by your own intellect.

Most things I don't even pray about anymore. I just say the word. If I need money I say, "Angels go out and cause the money to come in in the name of Jesus." I tell Satan to take his hands off of my money and the money comes in.

"Angels are ministering spirits, sent forth to minister for them who shall be heirs of salvation" *(Hebrews 1:14).*

I'm an heir!

You don't even have to pray, you can *say it.* If you believe it in your heart — without doubting — you can *SAY IT!*

So if you can tell a mountain to move — the biggest mountain I know *of* is Mt. Everest. It is approximately 29,000 feet high. That's over five miles high. That's a big mountain — brother — a big one! But Jesus said you can speak the word and say "move" and it will move.

You say, "Do you really believe that?"

Yes, I do! I believe that if the occasion arises, and I need a mountain to move, it will move.

This method — JUST SAYING IT with your mouth — not even praying about it—*JUST SAYING IT WITH YOUR MOUTH* — you shall have whatsoever you say — if you believe it in your heart — without doubting. *YOU CAN SAY IT!*

By just opening your mouth and saying, "Bless God, I believe that I receive my healing; I believe this tumor leaves now; I believe this cancer is cursed right now; I believe my needs are met right now; I believe this cataract has disintegrated right now; I believe that my ears are open right now; I believe it is so."

One night I was on Channel 40 (television Los Angeles) and they had me pray.

I said, "Anybody who is sick, lay your hands on that part of your body."

There was a deaf man, and he laid his hands on his ears, and he called in saying that when he put his hands on his ears, his ears were opened, as I prayed.

See, he did what the Word said.

I didn't do anything; *the Word did it. he believed it*, and his *faith was in action.*

Jesus said, you don't even have to pray, you can say it. Bless God it is so!

Friends, I hope you can see that I am giving you *what the Bible says.* Many people say that they can't understand the Bible.

That is the biggest lie that was ever told.

What good is the Bible if you can't understand it? What do you need it for if you can't understand it?

Who needs a car that won't run, a house that you can't live in, food that you can't eat, money that you can't spend? That's stupid.

Bless God, you can understand it, but you have to put in a little time on it. It's just like anything else, if you want to get something out of the Bible, you must spend a little time in it — maybe even burn the *midnight oil.*

It is not going to fall on you like oranges off of a tree, but I'm here to tell you that it works.

Now watch this, scripturally, *"And when Jesus was entered into Capernaum, there came unto him a centurion, beseeching him, and saying, Lord my servant lieth at home sick of the palsy, grievously tormented. And Jesus saith unto him, I will come and heal him. The centurion answered and said, Lord, I am not worthy that thou shouldest come under my roof: but speak the word only, and my servant shall be healed. For I am a man under authority, having soldiers under me: and I say to this man, Go, and he goeth; and to another Come, and he cometh; and to my servant, Do this and he doeth it. When Jesus heard it, he marvelled and said to them that followed, Verily I say unto you, I have not found so great faith, no, not in Israel. And I say unto you, That many shall come from the east and west, and shall sit down with Abraham, and Isaac, and Jacob, in the kingdom of heaven. But the children of the kingdom shall be cast out into outer darkness: there shall be weeping and gnashing of teeth. And Jesus said unto the centurion, Go thy way; and*

as thou hast believed, so be it done unto thee. And his ser-
vant was healed in the self-same hour" (Matthew 8:5-13).

Why was the servant healed?

Because that man *believed in his heart that what he said*
with *his mouth* would come to pass. He did just what Jesus
said.

Jesus said, *"Whosoever shall say unto this mountain be*
thou removed and be thou cast into the sea and shall not
doubt in his heart, but shall believe those things which he
saith, (THOSE THINGS WHICH HE SAITH, THOSE
THINGS WHICH HE SAITH) shall come to pass, he shall
have whatsoever he saith" (Mark 11:23).

Now understand friends, these verses in this Bible are
written to God's children. Don't think that as a child of the
Devil you can go out and make it work for you, because
it won't.

It is only for those in the family. "All In The Family,
Baby." All in the family.

Now notice what the centurion said in his confession
of faith. *"The centurion answered and said, Lord, I am not*
worthy that thou shouldest come under my roof, but speak
the word only, and my servant shall be healed."

See, he believed what he said. He said, "You don't even
have to come to my house, just say the word and he will be
healed." *HE BELIEVED WHAT JESUS SAID.* And Jesus
said he had great faith.

He didn't pray, the centurion just said, "Just speak the
Word, and my servant shall be healed".

The WORD says, "In that self-same hour (not next
month or next year, but in that self-same hour) the servant
was healed."

This is method number six — *"JUST BY SAYING IT;*
you don't have to pray, *JUST SAY IT.* But you must *BE-*
LIEVE IT IN YOUR HEART, not in your head, nct with
your intellect, not with that little gray matter you have up
there, not with that little *pea sized brain* sitting there be-

tween your shoulder blades. YOU MUST BELIEVE IT DOWN IN YOUR HEART — DOWN IN YOUR SPIRIT.

The only people who can believe *that* are those who have been born again, because the *new birth* is the *rebirth of the human spirit.* If you have never been born again, you are not *even* a child of God. If you are not a child of God, you can't believe God's Word, and if you can't believe God's Word, you are not going to receive God's blessings.

Only *my kids* get the benefit of the money I make. I don't take care of anybody elses children. My kids are in the family and they get the benefits of it.

We read a part of this Scripture in talking about the woman who touched Jesus' clothes, but we want to go back and *see* a different aspect. *"And a certain woman which had an issue of blood twelve years, and had suffered many things of many physicians, and had spent all that she had, and was nothing bettered, but rather grew worse, When she had heard of Jesus, came in the press behind, and touched his garment.* (WHY IN THE WORLD WOULD SHE DO A SILLY THING LIKE THAT? WHAT IN THE WORLD WOULD MAKE HER THINK THAT SHE COULD GET HEALED BY TOUCHING SOMEBODY'S GARMENT? — Jesus *said* you will have what you say.) *For she said,* (FOR SHE SAID) *if I can but touch his clothes I SHALL BE WHOLE"* (Mark 5:25-28).

Bless God! She touched Him and was made whole. Why was she made whole? Because she *believed in her heart* that *what she said with her mouth would come to pass.*

Jesus said, "Whosoever shall say, (whosoever shall say — *WHOSOEVER SHALL SAY*) unto this mountain, Be thou removed and be thou *cast into the sea; and shall not doubt* in his heart, but shall believe that those things which he saith shall come to pass, he shall have whatsoever he saith" *(Mark 11:23).* Whosoever shall say, Whosoever shall say, WHOSOEVER SHALL SAY.

SHE SAID IT — AND SHE DID IT — AND SHE GOT IT!

She didn't pray — *SHE JUST SAID IT AND SHE RECEIVED!*

JUST SAY IT.

METHOD NO. 7. WHEN YOU PRAY — BELIEVE THAT YOU RECEIVE IT

This seventh method of receiving healing — I believe is the highest kind of faith — is the highest way to receive healing.

Jesus is speaking here and He says, *"Therefore I say unto you, What things soever ye desire, when ye pray, believe that ye receive them, and ye shall have them"* (Mark 11:24).

Well, is Jesus a liar or does He tell the truth?

He tells the truth! He says, *"What things soever ye desire."*

Wouldn't that have to include healing? Doesn't that include bodily healing?

It must be God's will to heal then. Otherwise He could not make that kind of bold declaration. *"What things soever you desire WHEN YOU PRAY"* — not after you pray, not a month later, not when you see something, not when you understand it, but *"WHEN YOU PRAY BELIEVE THAT YOU RECEIVE IT?"*

If you believe you receive it, you will confess that, "Bless God — I believe I am healed, I believe I have received my healing."

Somebody says, "Yes, but you don't look like you are healed."

I didn't say, "I look like I'm healed," I said, *"I BELIEVE THAT I RECEIVED MY HEALING."*

"Yes, but how do you feel?"

"Bless God, I am not going by how I feel — I am going by what I believe — and I BELIEVE I AM HEALED."

"Yes, but that doesn't make sense."

"That's right, it is *not sense, it's faith.*"

"Yes, but that's illogical."

"You're right, *it's not logic, it's faith.*"

"Yes, but I just don't understand that."

"You're right, I don't understand it either, but I believe it."

I don't understand television, but I believe if I turn it on, I can look at a picture, but I don't understand the first thing about it, do you?

I don't understand how a gasoline engine works, how it works inside without blowing up the whole thing, but it pushes a piston down and drives a crank-shaft and turns a drive-shaft to the rear wheels, and turns the wheels when you put it in gear, and the car goes forward. I don't understand it, but I could care less — I know that when I turn that thing on and put it in gear, it is going and that is all that I'm concerned about.

I don't know how an airplane stays up in the sky, as big as a 747 is — that thing is gigantic. How does it stay up in the air?

I can't see the air, I can't touch the air. But I don't have to understand it to get on that plane and fly from the United States to Mexico, or to Hawaii, or somewhere else.

All I have to do is believe it, and get on board and go.

You don't have to understand how it works, just do what He says and you will get it, and after all, that is what you want anyway (the result — isn't it?).

PRAISE GOD! YOU DON'T HAVE TO DO ANY MORE THAN BELIEVE THAT YOU RECEIVE IT — and you shall have it!

IS HEALING FOR ALL?

I believe that it is so. I believe that I can walk in divine health all the days of my life.

You are reading after one man who will never be sick and I'm not being presumptuous.

If I'm reading my Bible right it says, *"He that dwelleth in the secret place of the most high, shall abide under the shadow of the Almighty"* (Psalms 91:1).

I'm right in there under His right wing — right up under that wing. God Himself said, *". . . neither shall any plague come nigh thy dwelling"* (Psalms 91:10). (Whose dwelling?) *"He that dwelleth in the secret place of the most high."*

What is plague? Isn't that sickness and disease?"

He said, "No plague will come nigh thy dwelling."

Well, I guess God lied!

NO! He went on to say, in verse 14, "With long life (not short life) will I satisfy him and show him my salvation."

PRAISE GOD! HEALING IS FOR ALL!

THANK GOD FOR SEVEN SCRIPTURAL WAYS TO RECEIVE HEALING!

Oh, that's not to say I'm not attacked. I'm attacked. The devil just sits like a blood hound — every morning I wake up he's sitting right on the foot of the bed. Sometimes he throws that dart right away, but it doesn't stop me, and it won't stop me, because I'm being strong — not in Fred Price — but I'm being "strong in the Lord and in the power of His might."

ALL RIGHT, we have studied the *SEVEN SCRIPTURAL WAYS OR METHODS TO RECEIVE HEALING.* Certainly you can find in these at least one way whereby you can receive your healing.

Just to refresh your memory, let's review briefly these seven ways, or methods, whereby you can receive healing.

NO. 1. "ANOINT WITH OIL"

"Is any sick among you? let him call for the elders of the church; and let them pray over him, anointing him with oil in the name of the Lord: and the prayer of faith shall save

the sick, and the Lord shall raise him up; and if he hath committed sins, they shall be forgiven him. Confess your faults
one to another, and pray one for another, that ye may be
healed. The effectual fervent prayer of a righteous man
availeth much" (James 5:14-16).

This method is for the very weak or feeble in faith. He
can see, touch or feel the oil and release his faith in the oil.
It is not the oil that heals; but it is *the oil* that *releases his
faith* in the *prayers of the righteous, and they will avail
much.*

NO. 2. "IF TWO OF YOU SHALL AGREE ON EARTH AS TOUCHING ANYTHING"

*"Again I say unto you, That if two of you shall agree on
earth as touching anything that they shall ask, it shall be
done for them of my Father which is in heaven. For where
two or three are gathered together in my name, there am I
in the midst of them"* (Matthew 18:19-20).

Literally — in the Greek — Jesus says, "Wherever two
or three are gathered together, there am I in the midst of
them to make good that that they have agreed upon."

Make sure you agree. Be sure you find out what they
are agreeing to.

NO. 3. LAYING ON OF HANDS

*"And these signs shall follow them that believe, in my
name they shall cast out devils; they shall speak with new
tongues; They shall take up serpents; and if they drink any
deadly thing, it shall not hurt them; They shall lay hands on
the sick, and they shall recover"* (Mark 16:17-18).

Jesus said, "THEY SHALL LAY HANDS ON THE
SICK AND THEY SHALL RECOVER."

Laying on of hands is Scriptural, you can receive your
healing this way.

NO. 4. GIFTS OF HEALINGS

*"For to one is given by the Spirit the word of wisdom,
to another the word of knowledge by the same Spirit; to*

another faith by the same Spirit; to another gifts of healing by the same Spirit: To another the working of miracles; to another prophecy, to another discerning of spirits, to another divers kinds of tongues; to another the interpretation of tongues: But all these worketh that one and the selfsame Spirit, dividing to every man severally as he will (I Corinthians 12: 8-11).

"And God hath set some in the church, first apostles, secondarily prophets, thirdly teachers, after that miracles then gifts of healings . . ." (I Corinthians 12:28).

GIFTS OF HEALINGS do not operate at the will of man, but as the Spirit wills. GIFTS OF HEALINGS will heal people — whether they are saints or sinners. They are actually and primarily for the unbelieving. It is really to attract attention to the POWER OF GOD.

For example, Kathryn Kuhlman's services attracts sinners and when people are being healed she gives out an invitation and all manner of people get saved.

NO. 5. SPECIAL ANOINTINGS

"And God wrought special miracles by the hands of Paul: so that from his body were brought unto the sick handkerchiefs or aprons, and the diseases departed from them, and the evil spirits went out of them" (Acts 19:11-12).

God wrought special miracles by the hands of Paul.

God wrought special miracles by the hands of Jesus. *"How God anointed Jesus of Nazareth with the Holy Ghost and with power" (Acts 10:38).*

Here is an account of how this special anointing worked in the ministry of Jesus, *"And a certain woman, which had an issue of blood 12 years, and had suffered many things of many physicians, and had spent all she had, and was nothing bettered, but rather grew worse. When she had heard of Jesus, came in the press behind, and touched his garments. For she said if I may touch but his clothes I shall be whole. And straightway the fountain of her blood was dried up; and she felt in her body that she was healed of that plague.*

And Jesus immediately knowing in himself that virtue (power) had gone out of him turned him about in the press and said, Who touched my clothes? (the Bible says that power went out of Jesus) *And his disciples said unto him, Thou seest the multitude thronging thee and sayest thou, Who touched me? And he looked around about to see her that had done this thing, But the woman fearing and trembling, knowing what was done in her, came and fell down before him and told him all the truth. And he said unto her, Daughter, thy faith hath made thee whole; go in peace and be whole of thy plague"* (Mark 5:25-34).

On God's side, the power went out of Jesus, on man's side her faith ignited that power.

Her faith was the match that made that power explode in her body.

That power was in Jesus' body and by *osmosis*: it just *crept out of His body, into His clothes*, and *all she did was touch His clothes.*

Oral Roberts and Kenneth Hagin have this *SPECIAL ANOINTING* from God. This is not an ordinary anointing for ordinary miracles, but it is a SPECIAL ANOINTING for *special miracles.*

Everybody won't have this gift, but everybody God wants to have it will have it.

These last two methods are covered in this chapter.

NO. 6. JUST SAYING IT

In this method, Say it with your mouth — not even praying about it. Mark 11:23 says, *"For verily I say unto you, That whosoever shall say unto this mountain, Be thou removed, and be thou cast into the sea; and shall not doubt in his heart, but shall believe that those things which he saith shall come to pass; he shall have whatsoever he saith."*

If you do not doubt in your heart but believe that those things you say with your mouth will come to pass, "Ye shall have *WHATSOEVER YE SAITH."*

NO. 7. WHEN YOU PRAY BELIEVE THAT YOU RECEIVE IT

Jesus says, *"Therefore I say unto you, what things soever ye desire, when ye pray, believe that ye receive them, and ye shall have them"* (Mark 11:24).

"WHAT THINGS SOEVER YE DESIRE" includes healing.

Certainly we have not exhausted the subject, but I believe what I have said about these SEVEN WAYS TO SCRIPTURAL HEALING — will give you valuable insights into the subject of divine healing.

IS HEALING FOR ALL?

I BELIEVE HEALING IS FOR ALL!

TO GOD BE THE GLORY!

7

Is God Glorified Through Sickness?

Part 1

One thing is evident, wherever you go on the face of Planet Earth, multitudes of people are sick and afflicted. Not only in the world, but also, more tragic than that, we see the *body of Christ* decimated with debilitating disease, sickness, and infirmity on every hand.

Whether you are a black Christian, a white Christian, a red Christian, or a yellow Christian, sickness and disease is *no respector of persons*. We are all afflicted alike.

There is much misunderstanding about sickness and disease and about God's place in it. Many accuse our Heavenly Father of making or causing people to be sick. They say that "God is teaching them something — that He's bringing them through the *'fiery furnace'* and is making better people out of them."

That sounds plausible, but is that Scripturally true?

I am interested and concerned about what *"thus saith the Lord,"* I have found that *freedom* comes from knowing the will of my heavenly Father. I could care less what your church thinks, or my church thinks, or what *"they say"*. I'm concerned only with *WHAT THE WORD SAYS.*

I believe in the WORDS OF JESUS CHRIST when He said in the Gospel of *John 8:31-32*, *". . . if you continue in my Word, then are you my disciples indeed, and you shall know the truth, and the truth shall make you free."*

I believe that nothing holds people in greater bondage than physical sickness and disease. I know there are other things, but now I am specifically interested in physical and bodily healing.

"IS GOD GLORIFIED THROUGH SICKNESS?"

I want to proceed by the inspiration and direction of the Holy Spirit to answer that question, in line with the Bible.

A ROPE OF SCRIPTURE —

By now you know that the Bible said in the "mouth of two or three witnesses let every word be established" (Matthew 18:16).

I propose to give you nine witnesses, not two or three, but nine. Enough for you to wrap the *rope of Scripture* around your neck and choke the unbelief out of you.

I know that there are some *die-hards* who will continue just as they were before reading this book. It isn't for you anyway! This book is only for *him who has ears to hear.* Praise God.

I ask you again — *"IS GOD GLORIFIED THROUGH SICKNESS?"*

Now it is one thing to *say no*, and it's another to *say yes.* But are you basing your answer on the Scripture? Can you give me chapter and verse?

See, that's a different thing. I can think that God is "*glorified through sickness*", or I can think that "*God is not glorified through sickness*".

Proponents of sickness and disease say, "God is responsible, and God is glorified through sickness." They are saying *that* out of their human mind and out of human experience.

Those who say, "*God is not glorified through sickness*" are saying *that* because of their great love and devotion to God. They can't reconcile it with God being a *God of love* that He would make people sick.

But you see, friend, the only thing that's going to stand the *acid test of time* is the WORD — THE WORD OF GOD. We want to go through the Word and find out what the Bible says about this.

Many of you who read this book live in many different areas of the country. You go to different churches, belong to different denominations. There will be sick people wherever you go. Right now you may think of certain ones you know, and perhaps love, who are sick. Some have already *passed on,* and you knew they loved the Lord, yet they died.

The question arose when the minister stood in the pulpit at the time of the funeral and said, "*The Lord gave and the Lord hath taken away, blessed be the name of the Lord*" (Job 1:21). "*IS GOD GLORIFIED THROUGH SICKNESS?*"

In chapter one of this book we established that sickness and disease *do not* originate with God. We established — from the Word of God — that Satan is the author of sickness and disease.

For example, you will remember in Acts Chapter 10 where Peter the apostle was at Simon the tanner's house. Peter went up on top of the house — for meditation and prayer — while the midday meal was being prepared. While he was there, on the roof-top, he fell into a trance. God let a sheet down from Heaven, and Peter saw a vision. God directed him to go to a Gentile man named Cornelius. Although Peter wasn't sure why he was to go, he followed and obeyed the leading of the Spirit.

Once upon the scene of Cornelius' house he began to question, "Why did you call for me?"

The man said, "I was praying one day, and had a vision. An angel appeared before me, and told me to send to Joppa, to Simon the tanner's house, for a man named Peter, and he'd come and tell me words whereby I and my house would be saved."

Then Peter said, "I perceive that God is no respector of persons, but that in every land and every nation, he that seeketh God, God will meet that man right there — at that point".

Then in the course of his discourse Peter made a very illuminating statement concerning the ministry of the Lord Jesus Christ.

I will remind you again, Peter was one of the "Big Three". Peter, James, and John were the *cabinet* of Jesus. They were in every high level meeting. Anytime a major decision was to be made, a particular direction to be approached, Jesus would call *in* Peter, James, and John. If anybody should know what Jesus' attitude was about sickness, disease and its origin, and whether God is glorified through sickness or not, Peter would know He traveled with Jesus for three and one-half years.

Let's hear from the mouth of Peter himself, what he came to know and realize about Jesus' attitude concerning sickness and disease and its origin. Peter said, *"How God anointed Jesus of Nazareth with the Holy Ghost and with power: who went about doing good and healing all that were oppressed of the devil" (Acts 10:38).*

Now I take it from that that Peter is giving us a capsulized view of the healing ministry of Jesus. He said that everybody that Jesus healed was *Satanically oppressed.* I didn't say *possessed* and I didn't say *obsessed,* I said OPPRESSED. Peter said that "Jesus went about healing all that were OPPRESSED OF THE DEVIL."

Now if that statement is to give us any indication of the magnitude and scope of the healing ministry of Jesus, then we must conclude that it covered the entire healing ministry —or else, it didn't give us an accurate account of the *healing ministry of Jesus.* I take it then that everybody that Jesus healed was Satanically oppressed.

Concluding from that, then, both Peter and Jesus understood that the *oppressor was Satan,* and the *deliverer* was *JESUS.*

Let's look at *Luke 13:10-16; again, "And he was teaching in one of the synagogues on the sabbath. And, behold, there was a woman which had a spirit of infirmity eighteen years, and was bowed together, and could in no wise lift up herself. And when Jesus saw her, he called her to him and said unto her, Woman, thou art loosed from thine infirmity. And he laid his hands on her: and immediately she was made straight, and glorified God."* Isn't that tragic? Bound for 18 long years, perhaps *rheumatoid arthritis,* or some disease or crippling infirmity like that. And isn't that nice that God did that to her so He could get glory from it? Let's follow on, *"And the ruler of the synagogue answered with indignation, because that Jesus had healed on the sabbath day, and said unto the people, There are six days in which men ought to work: in them therefore come and be healed, and not on the sabbath day. The Lord then answered him, and said, Thou hypocrite, doth not each one of you on the sabbath loose his ox or his ass from the stall, and lead him away to watering?"* Now watch this 16th verse, here's revelation for you. *"And ought not this woman, being a daughter of Abraham, whom Satan hath bound, lo these eighteen years, be loosed from this bond on the sabbath day?"*

Jesus said that Satan had her bound, and Jesus said because she was a daughter of Abraham, she ought to be free, and bless God, HE SET HER FREE!

I repeat, the above scripture shows that Satan is the one who brings infirmity upon people. Surely God and Satan couldn't be working hand in hand.

With that in mind, let's start answering the question, "IS GOD GLORIFIED THROUGH SICKNESS?" Let's see what the Bible says. We will read some Scripture together and you be the judge.

YOU BE THE JUDGE —

Let's read, *"And He entered into a ship, and passed over, and came into his own city. And, behold, they brought to him a man sick of the palsy, lying on a bed: And Jesus seeing their faith said unto the sick of the palsy; Son, be of good cheer; thy sins be forgiven thee. And behold, certain of the scribes said within themselves, This man blasphemeth. And Jesus knowing their thoughts said, Wherefore think ye evil in your hearts? For whether is easier, to say, Thy sins be forgiven thee; or to say, Arise, and walk? But that ye may know that the Son of man hath power on earth to forgive sins, (then saith he to the sick of the palsy,) Arise, take up thy bed, and go unto thine house. And he arose, and departed to his house. But when the multitudes saw it, they marvelled, and glorified God, which had given such power unto men"* *(Matthew 9:1-8).*

Now while the man was on the bed of affliction, a palsy victim, it doesn't indicate that God received any glory. But as soon as the man picked up his bed, and arose and went to his own house, the people marvelled at that. It blew their minds — in modern terminology. And it said — THEY GLORIFIED GOD.

When did they glorify him?

After that the man arose, healed, and went into his own house. Not while he was sick. Not while he was an invalid, lying on that couch. But, the moment the man was delivered, the moment the man was healed, *THEY GAVE GOD GLORY!*

"IS GOD GLORIFIED THROUGH SICKNESS?" Well it looks like in that case God received the glory, when the man was healed — not while he was sick.

Matthew 15:29-31 says, *"And Jesus departed from thence, and came nigh unto the sea of Galilee; and went up into a mountain, and sat down there. And great multitudes came unto him, having with them those that were lame, dumb, maimed, and many others, and cast them down at Jesus' feet; and he healed them:"* (Them who? Them lame, them blind, them dumb, them maimed, and many others.) *"Insomuch that the multitude wondered, when they saw the dumb to speak the maimed to be whole, the lame to walk, and the blind to see: and they glorified the God of Israel."*

When did they glorify Him?

They glorified Him after the lame walked, and the blind saw.

Is that right?

They didn't give Him any glory while the people were bound — crippled, and blind — but when they saw the lame to walk, the blind to see, and the maimed to be made whole — THEY GLORIFIED THE GOD OF ISRAEL!

It doesn't look like God received any glory while the folks were bound, does it?

HE WAS GLORIFIED WHEN THEY WERE HEALED!

Is that right? How readest thou?

Well I wonder, "IS GOD GLORIFIED THOUGH SICKNESS, AND DISEASE?" Or is He glorified when folks get healed?

All right, let's go on, we want to go through this a little more in detail. "Is God glorified through sickness?"

Remember the account in Luke 13:10-16. We studied about the woman who had a spirit of infirmity earlier in this same chapter. She was bowed together and could in no wise lift up herself. Then in the 12th and 13th verses Jesus called her, laid his hands on her and she was immediately made straight.

After she was made straight, in the 13th verse, what did she do?

She glorified God!

When?

When she was made straight!

It doesn't give any indication that, during the 18 years she was on *that afflicted list,* bowed together and could in no wise lift up herself, she gave God any glory. God *didn't get any glory* from her during that 18 years, but the first thing that popped out of the woman's mouth when she was healed was "Praise God!"

The Bible said Jesus laid His hands on her and said, "Woman thou art loosed," and immediately she was made straight — *AND GLORIFIED GOD!*

You say, "Well, we don't teach it like that in our church."

Well, thanks be to God, your church is not the Word of God, because we would be *"up the creek"* if it were.

Read with me Luke 17:11-13, *"And it came to pass, as he went to Jerusalem, that he passed through the midst of Samaria and Galilee. And as he entered into a certain village, there met him ten men that were lepers, which stood afar off: And they lifted up their voices, and said, Jesus, Master, have mercy on us."* Oh how pathetic and pitiful leprosy is. These people were required by the law of Moses to live in isolated encampments or places by themselves. It was forbidden for them to enter into the *main stream* of society, for this disease was quite contagious. And they were required — if they saw anybody at a distance, they were to cry out — "unclean, unclean." That would let the people know that they were *lepers,* and to stay their distance.

Verse 14 says, *"And when he saw them, he said unto them, Go shew yourselves unto the priests."* I want to show you something here about faith. The Lord uses me quite often in teaching on the subject of faith. I want you to notice that according to the law of Moses, if a man ever recovered from leprosy, if leprosy departed from his body, that man was required by the law of Moses to go to the high priest, so that the high priest could certify that the man was indeed and in fact clean. The high priest would then make an announcement to the people, and this man could then be re-introduced into *society*. Please notice, he had to go to the high priest first. He didn't go to the high priest until *after* the leprosy had departed from him.

Now I want you to notice that while these men were still leprous, while the leprosy was still there, Jesus said, *"go shew yourselves to the priest."* You see, in the mind of Jesus, when Jesus spoke the words the men were healed. They were cleansed as far as God was concerned, because, according to the Word of God, in Romans 4:17 *". . . God calleth those things which be not as though they were."* That's faith talking. Jesus said, *"Go shew yourselves to the priest."* Now listen to this, *"and it came to pass, that as they went, they were cleansed. And one of them, when he saw that he was healed, turned back, and with a loud voice glorified God."* He didn't even do it sedately. He did it loudly, fanatically. WITH A LOUD VOICE HE GLORIFIED GOD.

When?

HE GLORIFIED GOD WHEN HE WAS HEALED! God received the *glory* when the man was healed, not while the man was a leper. Can you see it? The Bible said it. I didn't say it! I didn't write it!

Do you see my name in there? My name doesn't appear. The Bible said that the man gave God GLORY!

When?

When he was healed.

Well, I deduce from that, that God must get the glory when people get well, not while they're bound and sick.

"IS GOD GLORIFIED THROUGH SICKNESS?"

WALKING AND LEAPING AND PRAISING GOD —

"*Now Peter and John went up together into the temple at the hour of prayer, being the ninth hour. And a certain man lame from his mother's womb was carried, whom they laid daily at the gate of the temple which is called Beautiful, to ask alms of them that entered into the temple.*" Isn't that something? Here's a man bound from his mother's womb. Came out lame. Could never hold down a good job, the best he could do was sit on the corner with his tin cup *out*, asking for handouts from people. "*Who seeing Peter and John about to go into the temple asked an alm. And Peter, fastening his eyes upon him with John, said, Look on us. And he gave heed unto them, expecting to receive something of them. Then Peter said, Silver and gold have I none; but such as I have give I thee: In the name of Jesus Christ of Nazareth rise up and walk. And he took him by the right hand, and lifted him up: and immediately his feet and ankle bones received strength. And he leaping up stood, and walked, and entered with them into the temple, walking, and leaping, and praising God*" (Acts 3:1-8).

He wasn't praising God while he was sitting there with that tin cup in his hand. No, all he could say was, "alms for the poor, alms for the poor, can you help a poor lame man please, I can't work, I don't have a job, will you please help me? Alms for the poor."

Bless God, when that man was healed, the Bible says that he "*LEAPED UP AND STOOD AND WALKED, LEAPING AND PRAISING GOD.*"

He wasn't asking for any more alms, He was saying, "Praise God, I'm healed!"

Let's read verse 9 of the same chapter. Now watch this, "*And all of the people saw him walking, and praising God.*"

Now we are going to see the *sequel* to this story. Because of the healing of the lame man, Peter and John were apprehended by the Sanhedrin Council. They were brought to task for teaching in the *"name of Jesus"*. They brought them before the *council*, harassed and bugged them, and tried to *trump up* charges against them. But, they could find no legal reason to hold them.

Notice in *Acts 4:21*, *"So when they had further threatened them, (the Sanhedrin Council) they let them go, finding nothing how they might punish them, because of the people: for all men glorified God for that which was done."*

"FOR ALL MEN GLORIFIED GOD FOR THAT WHICH WAS DONE."

They weren't even Christians. The sinners cried out and gave glory to God! because they saw that this was a mighty and stupendous act of Almighty God.

"They found nothing how they might punish them because of the people."

What people?

The people who were all around and saw the lame man healed. It didn't say "because of the Christians," it said "because of the people. For all men glorified God for that which was done."

What was done?

The man was healed so *God received glory* for the man getting healed.

Can you see it? *"IS GOD GLORIFIED THROUGH SICKNESS?"*

Well, so far we haven't found any place where the Bible says that God is *"glorified through sickness"*. In fact, every place we've looked thus far contradicts that *idea*.

Don't you realize just by common sense — that if there were some Scriptures that said, *"God was glorified through sickness"* it would contradict these Scriptures? And, that would invalidate the Bible. The Bible would contradict itself.

Chew on that a little bit . . . You'll get it!

All right, read with me, *"And it came to pass, that as he was come nigh unto Jericho, a certain blind man sat by the way side begging: And hearing the multitude pass by, he asked what it meant. And they told him, that Jesus of Nazareth passeth by. And he cried, saying, Jesus, thou son of David, have mercy on me. And they which went before rebuked him, that he should hold his peace:* (Weren't they a loving bunch?) *but he cried so much the more, Thou son of David, have mercy on me. And Jesus stood, and commanded him to be brought unto him: and when he was come near, he asked him, Saying, What wilt thou that I shall do unto thee? And he said, Lord, that I may receive my sight. And Jesus said unto him, Receive thy sight: thy faith hath saved thee"* (Luke 18:35). Or healed thee. Verse 43 says, *"And immediately he received his sight, and followed him, glorifying God: and all the people, when they saw it, gave praise unto God."* "GAVE PRAISE UNTO GOD."

Not only did the man give Him glory, but also the people, when they saw it, they started praising God for it.

They weren't praising God while the man was blind. They were telling him to shut up, be quiet, don't trouble the master.

They were doing everything else but giving God glory. They were saying, in essence, "be quiet, don't trouble the master, he doesn't have time for you, keep your blindness." But when the man was healed, bless God, he gave God glory, and when the people saw what had happened — the man who was born blind was transformed, changed, and his eyes were suddenly opened — they knew that *that* was the power of Almighty God. They knew that *that* was — Jehovah Rapha — *"the Lord that healeth thee"* operating among His people in the land of Israel. And bless God, they gave Him praise and glory for it. Not while the man was blind, but when he was healed.

8

Is God Glorified Through Sickness? Part 2

"IS GOD GLORIFIED THROUGH SICKNESS?"

We don't want to be precipitous about answering the question. But, we want to go a little further and let the Word of God do it.

GLORIFY GOD IN THE TEMPLE —

Most of you who read this book go to church. Perhaps your church is large. Perhaps it has beautiful *stained glass windows.* I'm sure you think a lot of your *church building.* There is nothing wrong with that, as long as you don't worship the place. Then you enter into idolatry — but, I mean you consider and respect it as being God's house.

Some of you who smoke or drink and do other things, don't smoke or drink inside the main sanctuary of your church. You consider that a holy place, and you put your cigarettes *out* before you enter in. You wouldn't want to be caught smoking inside the church building because *"that's God's house."*

If you should walk into your church one Sunday morning and see a gaping hole in the ceiling with the rain falling through — you'd have a *fit.*

You'd say, "Why this is terrible, this is a disgrace before God. This is *God's house,* we ought to do better than this. All of the toilets are running over, the pipes are all broken, water is running all over the floor, this is a disgrace."

The beautiful *stained glass window* has a big hole in it.

You'd say, "Why this is terrible, we have to get that fixed."

The carpet's all moth-eaten, stringy, straggly, all discolored.

You wouldn't like that — would you?

You'd say, "That's a shame, Brother Price, we ought to do something about that, this is *'God's house.'* "

You'd have respect unto it, wouldn't you? You would want it fixed — that hole repaired, carpet fixed, that plumbing taken care of — wouldn't you?

Why?

"Because that's God's house."

All right now, just keep that in mind. I want to show you something. *"What? know ye not that your body is the temple of the Holy Ghost which is in you, which ye have of God, and ye are not your own? For ye are bought with a price: therefore glorify God in your body, and in your spirit, which are God's"* (I Corinthians 6:19-20).

GLORIFY GOD, GLORIFY GOD? WHERE? In the church building. In the closet, at the altar, at a retreat, or some camp, or some conference?

NO!

IT SAYS — GLORIFY GOD IN YOUR BODY, AND IN YOUR SPIRIT WHICH ARE GOD'S.

Now see, your body is the temple; your body is where God dwells. The Bible says that God does not live in houses made by men's hands.

And yet you have respect unto your church-house; the first you-know-what church down on Main and so-and-so street. You'd have a fit if you drove up to it and saw one of those *stained glass windows* broken. You'd want it fixed immediately, because it would be a disgrace before God, because you *consider* that God's house.

It is not *even* God's house.

GOD'S HOUSE IS YOUR BODY, but you don't mind if the windows are knocked out of this house. You don't mind if the plumbing doesn't work in this house, you don't mind if the organs don't work in this house. because it's just an old broken-down body. It doesn't have any significance at all, but God forbid that we should let this brick and mortar building go to deterioration. Because that's the house of God.

Is it?

We just read it — *your body is the temple of God.* If you wouldn't allow that crap and corruption in the physical building that you call a church, why do you think that God wants it inside of your body? That's where He lives. Who thinks that God wants to live in a house that He can't see out of the windows, He can't hear out of the ears, He can't walk with the legs, and He can't move the hands?

Your body is the temple. This — my body, (your body) — is the temple. Praise God! God dwells in your body!

He said, "I'll walk in them, I'll live in them. And they shall be my people, and I will be their God."

And yet we have a fit over that brick and mortar and lie down like whipped dogs when Satan puts some affliction or infirmity on us. We have the audacity to say, "It's for the glory of God."

Why don't you break all the windows out of the church building for the glory of God, then? You wouldn't want the people around the neighborhood to see it. You'd be ashamed of it. But you're not ashamed for them to see the place that God has created to *dwell in* broken, in a wheel chair, or on a bed of affliction.

Are you seeing anything here?

"IS GOD GLORIFIED THROUGH SICKNESS?"

Let's look in the Word of God. I want you to notice, we have just been reading the WORD. I've given you *clear scripture* — the Word of God.

If you reject anything, you're rejecting God's Word.

You're not rejecting me.

Let's look at this, *"And it came to pass the day after, that he went into a city called Nain; and many of his disciples went with him, and much people. Now when he came nigh to the gate of the city, behold, there was a dead man carried out, the only son of his mother, and she was a widow: and much people of the city was with her. And when the Lord saw her, he had compassion on her, and said unto her, Weep not. And he came and touched the bier: and they that bare him stood still. And he said, Young man, I say unto thee, Arise. And he that was dead sat up, and began to speak. And he delivered him to his mother. And there came a fear on all: and they glorified God, saying, That a great prophet is risen up among us; and, That God hath visited his people"* Luke 7:11-16.

This young man was *too young to die.* Do you know that in all of the accounts that we have in the Bible of Jesus raising the dead *He always raised young people?* Did you ever think about that?

Your minimum days should be seventy years, that's just the bare minimum. You ought to live to be at least 120 years of age. That's the Bible. God out of His own mouth — in the Old Testament — said the number of your days shall be 120 years.

I didn't write it!

God said it. The minimum ought to be 70 years, and you shouldn't go out with sickness or disease then.

So Jesus raised this man up. Perhaps he'd been sick and he had died.

When the people saw what happened, they did what?

They glorified God! *GLORIFIED GOD!*

When?

After the man was raised up. Are you following? After the man was raised.

"IS GOD GLORIFIED THROUGH SICKNESS?"

It looks like — *He's not!*

I mean, if God's going to be fair about this, don't you think that *just one place, just one time,* there should be one incident somewhere in the ministry of the Lord Jesus Christ where Jesus told somebody to stay *"sick for the glory of God"?*

I'm not asking for ten or fifteen — *just one time* — at least, to buttress up *this lie — spawned in the pit of hell —* that it's God's will — and that God is glorified through sickness and disease.

Did you know that there's not one single account in the four Gospels under the ministry of Jesus where Jesus *ever* told anybody to stay sick — *not one time.*

THE LAST CRUTCH —

Now I'm going to knock the *last crutch* from under you!

Somebody will say again, "Well, Brother Price, what about the man born blind, didn't Jesus say that he was sick for the glory of God?"

No, We talked about this in chapter one of this book, but to refresh your memory, we will look at it again.

"And as Jesus passed by, he saw a man which was blind from his birth. And his disciples asked him, saying, Master, who did sin, this man, or his parents, that he was born blind? Jesus answered, Neither hath this man sinned, nor his parents: but that the works of God should be made manifest in him. I must work the works of him that sent me, while it is day: the night cometh, when no man can work. As long as I am in the world, I am the light of the world. When he had thus spoken, he spat on the ground, and made clay of the spittle, and he anointed the eyes of the blind man with the clay. And said unto him, Go, wash in the pool of Siloam, (which is by interpretation, Sent). He went his way therefore, and washed, and came seeing" (John 9:1-7).

You say, "I knew it! We got him now. I knew Brother Price was wrong all along. Notice what Jesus said, Jesus said the man was sick for the glory of God, the man was bound for the glory of God."

Let's go back and look at this again. Now you remember, I told you that when the New Testament was originally written it was written in *Greek* — not in *English* — and in its original writing it was wrtten in all capital letters. There were no punctuation marks, no chapter divisions, no verses. The chapter divisions, the verses, the capitalization, the punctuation, were added by the translators to render clarity. The WORDS ARE INSPIRED, but the punctuation, the capitalization, the verses and chapters are not inspired.

Again, I propose to rearrange the punctuation marks.

I *know* that he who *leaves out,* or *takes away,* or *adds to* the Bible is in *serious trouble.* I don't want to get in trouble. I'm not going to add one word or take away one word.

I do want to throw this out there for you. You are under no obligation to accept it, but I want you to *see* if you can't honestly see a difference when we rearrange the punctuation marks.

All right, with that in mind let's go through this again.

"And as Jesus passed by (comma), he saw a man which was blind from his birth (period). And his disciples asked him (comma), saying (comma), Master (comma), who did sin (comma), this man (comma), or his parents (comma), that he was born blind (question mark)?"

All right, they asked Jesus a two-fold question. They were saying, in essence, "the man is blind, that we can see, there's no doubt about that. What we want to know is what caused the man's blindness? Did the man sin or did the parents sin, what caused the man to be born blind?"

Notice this, they didn't ask Jesus did God make him blind. Isn't it interesting? They didn't say, *"Did God make him blind?"* They said, "did the parents do something to cause him to be born blind, or did the man himself do it?"

The Jews had the idea that a baby could sin inside of its mother's womb. That's why they asked if the man did something to make him blind.

All right, let's go to verse 3, "*Jesus answered (comma), Neither hath this man sinned (comma), nor his parents (period).* (That answered their question).

They said, "the man is blind, that we can see. What we want to know is who sinned?" That question — that two-fold question — is going to elicit from Jesus one of three answers — either the man, the parents, or neither. Jesus answered, neither the man nor his parents had sinned. Let's go on, we add a capital "B" to but, "*But that the works of God should be made manifest in him (comma), I must work the works of him that sent me.*" And Jesus proceeded to do the works.

What were the works?

To spit on the ground, to make some clay, to anoint his eyes, and to tell him to go to the pool of Siloam and wash it off.

The man went and washed, and came seeing, praise God!

JESUS DIDN'T SAY THAT THE WORK OF GOD WAS THAT THE MAN BE BLIND, for if that were the *work of God,* Jesus *violated His Father's works,* because *he healed the man.*

No, the work of God was THAT THE MAN BE MADE WHOLE! and Jesus set about to do the work. Jesus didn't say that the man was blind for the work of God. Jesus said, "THAT THE WORKS OF GOD MAY BE MANIFEST IN HIM." "I must do the works. If I don't do the works, the works of God won't be manifested in him."

I'm *here* to tell you, friend, that if *we* don't do the *works* of God, the works of God are not going to be manifested in the people of the world, for Jesus said in JOHN'S gospel, chapter 14, verse 12, ". . . *the works that I do shall he do also . . . because I go unto my Father.*"

We are supposed to do the works of Jesus, and what were the works of Jesus?

". . . *to preach deliverance to the captives, and recovering of sight to the blind, to set at liberty them that are bruised*" *(Luke 4:18).*

Praise God! *THAT'S THE WORD OF GOD!*

"IS GOD GLORIFIED THROUGH SICKNESS?"

It looks like he's not! Praise God!

Thank you Father for your *WORD.* For your *WORD IS TRUTH, AND YOUR WORD IS FREEDOM!*

The Bible says, *"Jesus Christ is the same yesterday, today, and for ever"* (Hebrews 13:8).

When Jesus walked the earth He was God incarnated in the flesh. And He went about doing good and healing everybody who was bound by sickness and disease; according to Peter, everybody that Jesus healed was *oppressed* by the devil.

Jesus Himself said that that woman who was bound for 18 long years should be free — yes, even on the sabbath day — because she was a daughter of Abraham; and the promise that God gave Abraham was riches and health.

If she was a daughter of Abraham and could get healed under the *old covenant,* bless God, we can be healed under the *new covenant!* (a better covenant).

Not one single person during the three and one-half years of the ministry of Jesus that He ever healed was a *born again person.* Nobody was *born again* until after Calvary. They were not *Christians* in the sense that we are Christians. They were Israelites, with the promise of hope of the coming of the Messiah. If they could get healed under the *old covenant,* I find the Bible saying to me that we have a *better covenant* — established upon *better promises.* So if we have a *better covenant,* it has to include everything in the *old covenant,* and then some more! Hallelujah! Praise God!

The Bible says, *"They who are of faith are the children of Abraham" (Galatians 3:7)*. Praise God! the blessings of Abraham belong to me! Christ has redeemed us from the curse of the law that the blessing of Abraham might come on us.

You'll find in the 28th chapter of Deuteronomy that the *curse of the law* was *sickness and disease,* and the *blessing* was *good health*. Hallelujah, I have it! I sure hope you do! Because it's available to you right now!

"IS GOD GLORIFIED THROUGH SICKNESS?"

Now it's true, friend, and I know what some of you are thinking. You're saying, "Yeah, Brother Price, I disagree with that. I remember my brother — bless his dear darling heart. He *loved* the Lord, and he had five brothers, they wouldn't even go to church. You couldn't get them near the church, but my brother was stricken with cancer, and at the early age of 47 years, he went to be with the Lord.

"At the funeral, all five of those boys got saved."

I've heard of that and thank God for that. But that wasn't *God's perfect will* that *that* brother die so that those other five boys could get saved.

It was God's perfect will that *HIS SON — JESUS — DIE SO THAT THOSE FIVE BOYS COULD GET SAVED.* I *know* that good has happened sometimes, you understand, as a result of Christians *dying*. But, that's not *God's best,* and why settle for one man who's 47 years old dying to get five people saved.

It is conceivable that if he had lived out just his minimum years, (70 years) he would have another 23 years — and bless God it is certainly conceivable that he could have influenced at least one person to *get saved,* or been instrumental in leading one person to Christ a year. That would have been 23 more people saved if he had lived than were saved by his dying.

Why settle for *less* when we can have the *best*?

Do you see what I mean?

Certainly, God can take anything that Satan does, and make good come out of it, but that's not God's best.

The Bible says, ". . . *All things work together for good to them that love God, to them that are called according to His purpose"* (Romans 8:28).

It didn't say *all things are good.* It said, "ALL THINGS WORK TOGETHER *FOR GOOD* TO THEM THAT LOVE GOD."

Here is a situation. A man is stricken with a paralytic disease; he's working on a particular job. All of the employees hear about him being stricken. One of the employees who is an *atheist* goes down to the hospital to visit this brother. This brother happens to be a *Christian.* There he is, *lying on this bed of affliction.* He's in a cast from his neck down, unable to move. All he can do is speak and roll his eyes.

The *atheist* comes *in* and says, "Why *hi,* John, I heard about this terrible thing that has come upon you. Gee — I'm really sorry about it."

That *guy* looking *up* from his *bed of affliction* says, "Yes, it's too bad, but I want to say this one thing. I know Jesus as my Lord, and I want to ask you, my co-worker, do you know Jesus as your Lord? I want to tell you that there is salvation for you if you'll come to the Lord Jesus Christ, and confess Him as the Lord of your life. Not only that, but you can have your sins forgiven, and you can look forward to going to Heaven. Not only that — you perhaps — can even look forward to a *bed of affliction* like mine."

I'm sure that man would say, "If that's what Jesus has to offer, I don't need it."

A few moments later another brother comes *in.* A Christian brother who had heard about this man's affliction. He strides into the room with a Bible in his hand, and says, "Brother, I heard about your affliction."

"Yes, I'm on this bed of *affliction. God is testing me.* I'm doing this for *the glory of God.*"

The man opens his Bible and says, "Brother, did you know that the Bible in Matthew 8:17 says, '. . . *that Himself took our (your) infirmities and bore our (your) sicknesses?*' "

"No, I didn't know that."

"Did you know, brother, that I Peter 2:24 says, '*Who his own self bare our sins in His own body on the tree, that we being dead to sin should live unto righteousness, by whose stripes ye were healed.*'?"

"Why no, I didn't know that."

"Well, brother, It's *God will* for you to be well. Do you want to *rise up off of that bed?*"

"Yes," he says. "Lay your hands on me."

This brother that has the Bible in one hand, lays the other hand on the afflicted man, and says, "IN THE NAME OF JESUS CHRIST OF NAZARETH, I bind this thing that has bound this man, and I loose him, in the Name of Jesus."

The power of God flows out of that man's hand into the afflicted man's body, and the man jumps off of that bed and the cast bursts from him and he starts dancing around the room, praising the Lord, and shouting the victory!

The other man, who is an *atheist,* turns with wide-eyed amazement, and says, "*take me to your leader!*"

I think *that* would have a greater effect on enticing a man to come to Christ, to *see* the power of God, than to see some debilitating sickness or disease killing a man.

"The works that I do, shall ye do also, because I go to my Father."

Praise God! *THAT'S THE WORD OF GOD!*

"IS GOD GLORIFIED THROUGH SICKNESS?"

What sayest thou?

I SAY NO! GOD IS NOT GLORIFIED THROUGH SICKNESS!

PRAISE THE LORD!

9

My Personal Testimony of Healing

When I was a young man of junior high school age, I contracted a growth in my chest cavity, about the size of a green pea. I didn't pay any attention to it as a kid. I just played and horsed around and did my thing, and didn't even think about it.

As time went on I married, and this growth had grown to the size of a quarter. As time passed it grew to the size of a silver dollar, and it began to press against the mammary gland. The pain was excruciating. It was as though someone would take an ice-pick and stick it right in your eyeball. Just the thought of *that* — that's how it felt. Just to lay my shirt or my coat against that section of my body would hurt.

At that time I didn't know that God would heal. They told me there was a *power-failure* in heaven. They told me *that* went *out* with the early church. They told me I was just supposed to suffer, tough it out, keep a stiff upper lip.

So I went to the doctor — thank God for doctors. I'm not opposed to doctors or medicine. Thank God for what man has been able to do to help himself. Doctors are fighting the same enemy that we are; the only difference *is* they're using *tooth-picks* and we are using *atomic bombs!* That's the difference. Please believe me, I don't mean to ridicule *medical science*. I thank God for them. I'm telling you, if it weren't for doctors, most Christians would be dead. That's right. You had better thank God for doctors. I am not opposed to medical science, don't misunderstand me, I don't mean to leave that impression. It's not *that*. There's just a better way.

My wife and I went from Los Angeles to Pittsburgh, Pennsylvania one time. We could have ridden a bicycle with a tandem car on the side, it's been done before. It's not impossible, but there's a better way. We boarded an L-1011 Jetliner and sat back and snoozed all the way. See, you can ride a bike, but why ride a bike when you can fly? Why have your insides cut out when you can be healed? That's all I'm saying.

Now if you don't have any faith, and you don't have Jesus, man, you had better find a doctor as fast as you can, because you're in trouble. Thank God they are available to us.

Well, I went to the surgeon. He examined me and said, "Yes — Mr. Price, you have a tumor — this kind is usually not malignant, but we're not sure. We'll have to go in and make a little incision and open it up and take out the tumor. It's just a minor thing."

Any time they put you to sleep and start cutting on you —that's not minor, that's MAJOR! They could cut your leg off, and you wouldn't even know it until it's *too late*.

But anyway, they operated and took the thing out and sewed me *back up*.

Later I went back to the doctor for a *check-up*, and the doctor said, "Well Mr. Price, everything is fine, it's not malignant. The flesh will *fill in* after a while, (fatty-tissue) and you won't even notice it. It'll just be a little scar, but one thing I will caution you about regarding this particular kind of *tumor* — sometimes vestiges of it remain in the body and may float over to the other side of your *chest-cavity* and begin to develop again; we're not sure, we're not certain, but I'm just forewarning you."

Time passed and as I was showering one day, I noticed a little knot under the skin. I didn't pay any attention to it at first, but finally that knot grew to the size of a dime, then the size of a nickel, then the size of a quarter; and then it was back to that silver-dollar size — and oh, that excruciating pain.

But now, Bless God, I knew what the Word said. I found out that the Bible said, *"Himself took my infirmities and bore my sickness" (Matthew 8:17).* I asked the question, "If He took them and bore them, why in the world would He want me to take them and bear them?" That wouldn't make sense.

Then I found that I Peter 2:24 said, *". . . with his stripes I was healed."* And I said, "If I was, I am, and if I am, I is!" I took my Bible and I stood up in my room in January of 1972 and I said, "Heavenly Father I want to call you into record — Jesus, I want to call you into record as a witness — Holy Spirit, I want to call you into record — angels of Heaven, I call you into record; Satan, demons, I call you into record — this day, that I take my stand on the *authority* of the written revealed Word of my Heavenly Father, I *believe* according to *Matthew 8:17* which says, '. . . *Himself took my infirmities and bore my sicknesses,*' (and that means Fred Price) and *I Peter 2:24* which says, '. . . *and with his stripes I was healed,*' (and that means Fred Price.)" I took *Mark 11:24* and I said, *"Jesus told me that what things soever I desire,* (and I desire that this tumor disappear) *He said what things soever ye desire when ye pray,* (and I am now praying) He said to *believe that I receive them,* (and I now believe that I receive them) and He said *that I shall have them,* (and I believe that I shall have them) and I thank you for it, and I count it as done."

That was January of 1972; nothing happened, in the natural.

January, February, March came, and the growth grew larger, and the pain grew worse.

April, May, and June — six months later, the growth grew larger, and the pain grew worse.

Every day during those six months in my prayer time I said, "Father, I thank you, I believe I'm healed."

See, I never said, "*I was healed.*" I never said I felt like it, I never said I looked like it, I said I believed it. "Father you told me that I was, and I believed what you said, so I believe that I am, and of course ". . . faith is the evidence of things not seen" Hebrews 11:1.

I had my *faith* until the manifestation came. When the manifestation comes, I don't need my faith any more. Do you understand that?

I was preaching on divine healing, I was preaching on the gifts of the spirit, you know, and Satan was screaming in my ear.

He said, "Fred Price, you are a *fanatic*, you're a *fool*, you're *out there* telling your congregation that God *heals*, and He still *works miracles*, look at your chest, feel it, touch it."

If Satan can keep you in the *sense realm*, he will destroy you — but if you keep him in the *faith realm*, you'll put him under your feet. I said, "devil, I didn't *say* I looked like I was healed; I didn't say I felt like I was healed. I said, I believe that I am healed on the authority of the Word of God, and the Bible said that not one jot, not one tittle, not one comma, question mark, semi-colon, or parenthesis, will pass out of His Word, until it's all fulfilled. God said, I'll watch over my Word, to perform it. My Word will not return unto me void. I have magnified my Word, even above my name." I said, "Devil, on the authority of the Word of God,

I believe that I am healed. I received it in January, and I believe I'm healed now."

July, August, September, the growth grew larger, and the pain grew worse. September, October, November, 11 months later, over 300 days.

Every day I said, "Lord, I thank you, I believe I'm healed."

I never did feel like it, but I never said I felt like it.

I said, "I believe I'm healed. Jesus told me, when I pray, believe that I receive, and I'd get it, and I believe it. Oh! I believe it."

I was prepared to stand there for 10,000 years, and if it didn't work, I was going to take my little bony, puny finger and put it in the face of God and tell Him, "your Word didn't work." Now that's not sacrilegious. See, the only thing that we can go on is what God says in His Word, and if His Word isn't any good — then God's not good. I mean — it's just like you — if I can't count on your word, I can't count on you, can I?

Have you ever seen God?

No!

But you have His Word, isn't that right?

Well, that Word is true.

November came, and I was showering — and soaping up that wash cloth and all of a sudden I got over to that section of the body and I didn't feel that usual pain, and I dropped that cloth and grabbed my chest and it was gone. It had disappeared! I'm healed now!

See, I don't *need* any faith now, I have the *real thing*. I have *the manifestation*. I don't need my faith for that anymore. "Faith is the evidence of things not seen."

When you see it, you don't need faith, until then it is your faith that gets it.

Somebody said, "Well — why did it take so long?"

Well I don't know, and I don't care. I GOT IT! He didn't tell you to ascertain the time of the manifestation, He told you to believe that you receive. And I'll tell you one thing, if you don't believe that you have received it, there won't be any manifestation. I believe the main reason there is a time lag from the time you claim your healing, until the manifestation comes, is because many times our faith is not sufficiently developed to grasp the Word of God with our hearts or spirits. We are really believing with our heads and not with our hearts. It takes a little time for it to go from our heads to our hearts. But, if we will keep confessing with our mouths what the Word says, we will soon school ourselves into faith. I was just a babe, at the time, concerning faith and I had to grow. I kept saying what the Word said, "I believe I'm healed." I kept saying it until it went from my head to my heart, and when it did, it exploded like a bomb. Now, since I've been using my faith regularly, it doesn't take that long for the manifestations to come. I can come against symptoms that Satan would try to put upon my body and in a matter of a day of two, 24 hours in most cases, all the symptoms are gone, praise God! Now I walk in divine health and SO CAN YOU!

Many are the days when I want to just stop and give it *up* in the natural. Many are the days when my body feels like it's been beaten with rubber hoses; many are the days when I have pain so bad and so severe and so sharp that I almost want to cry, and lie down, and play dead, but I won't give in to the devil. I'd rather curse than say I'm sick; I'd rather blaspheme God than to admit I'm sick. I'd rather spit before I'd say I'm sick, because when I say that I'm sick, then I'm slapping my Lord and Saviour right in His face, because the Bible says "that Himself took my infirmities, and bore my sicknesses, and with His stripes I was healed." If I say I'm not healed, then He died in vain, He bled for nothing.

The Bible says that Jesus became our surety of a better covenant. Jesus became sick for you. The Bible says in Isaiah, that on Calvary He was so disfigured, His body was so bent out of shape, His Spirit was so twisted, that He didn't even look like a man any more. Sin had crushed Him in His spirit; sickness and disease had taken hold of His body. He had cancer, tuberculosis, syphilis, gonorrhea, and everything else all at one time. All of it from the whole world, *came* on Him, and He took *everybody's* sickness, *everybody's* disease upon His own body, and the Bible says, He didn't even look like a human being anymore. He was totally disfigured.

And He did it for YOU, and for you to admit that you're sick is to slap Him in the face. I won't do that! He gave too much, and He didn't have to do it. It would have been different if He had to do it — *BUT HE DIDN'T HAVE TO DO IT*.

He could have said, "Let them go to hell — I don't care, let them burn for eternity, let them burn in the lake of fire. I'm not going to soil my Holy hands with the sin and degradation, the foolishness and prejudices and the stupidity of mankind — let them die."

But no, He said, "Father prepare me a body, I'll go down to Calvary's rugged brow, I'll give my life for them. I'll take all of the sickness — all of the sin — all of the diseases — and every wicked and lewd thing in the world — I'll take it upon me."

When you accept sickness, you're saying, "Jesus, you died in vain! You paid the price for nothing!"

I won't do it — I won't give the devil the satisfaction! I refuse to do it — I'd count myself as a *traitor* if I accepted sickness and disease. I Peter 2:24 says ". . . With his stripes ye were healed." If ye *WERE*, ye *ARE*, if ye *ARE*, ye *IS*. Praise God I *IS!* How about you?

10

How You Can Receive Healing By Faith

Now let's deal with something that affects our physical bodies. How to receive healing for your body by faith.

Again, every claim that we make must be based on the WRITTEN WORD OF GOD. A *faith claim* only has validity when it is grounded in the Scriptures.

The following examples are not the only scripture references in the Bible on healing. I'm just giving you a representative *few*.

(1) THE PRAYER: (the claiming of the promise of God relative to your healing.) "Heavenly Father, I thank you for your WORD. Based on your Word, which declares, in *Matthew 8:17, 'That it might be fulfilled which was spoken by Esaias the prophet, saying, Himself took our infirmities, and bare our sicknesses.'* And *I Peter 2:24* which says, *'Who his own self bare our sins in his own body on the tree, that we, being dead to sins, should live unto righteousness: by whose stripes ye were healed.'* "

Father, according to these verses of Scriptures, Jesus *took* and *bore* my sicknesses and diseases, and I Peter 2:24 says that with His stripes I *was* healed. *Took, bore,* and *was* (*were*) are all past tense terms, indicating that the time of the action has already taken place as far as you are concerned. Your Word further declares in Mark 11:24; *'Therefore I say unto you, What things soever ye desire, when ye pray, believe that you receive them, and ye shall have them.'*

Father, I desire to be healed. I desire this cancer to leave my body. You said *'what things soever ye desire.'* I desire to be healed. You said, *'When ye pray.'* I am now praying. You said, *'believe that ye receive them.'* I now believe that I receive my healing for this cancer, (heart trouble; bad eyes;

bad back; bad heart; etc. etc.) You said, '*and ye shall have them.*'

I believe I receive by faith, and *faith is my evidence,* according to Hebrews 11:1, '*Now faith is . . . the evidence of things not seen.*' By faith I have it. Therefore, it must come. Thank you Father, in Jesus name, I believe I'm healed."

(2) THE PRAYER (thanksgiving and confession).

"Father, I thank you in Jesus' name. I believe I have received my healing. I believe that I have it now."

This prayer is to be prayed *until the physical manifestation of the healing takes place in your body.*

Remember, you are *healed by faith,* and *not by sight. Faith* is the *evidence of the healing* — *not the fact* that the cancer has left your body. *Your confession, between the time that you pray and claim your healing until it is seen in your body, is what causes it to come.*

THIS IS FAITH HEALING — simply believing that you have received the healing because the *WORD OF GOD SAYS, "THAT WITH HIS STRIPES YE WERE (WERE) HEALED."* If you really believe that you are healed, you can see how *unbelieving it would be to pray for that healing again.* To pray again would be saying that you didn't get it the first time, because if you did get it the first time, there would be no need to pray the second time. Right?

Now your body may *scream louder than ever* that you are sick. Fever, pain, nausea, lumps, etc. This is where *your confession* comes in. YOU MUST CONFESS THE WORD OF GOD IN THE FACE OF EVERY SYMPTOM AND EVERY PAIN. This is *faith* versus *sense* knowledge.

Remember, Satan is the God of this world, which includes everything in the sense realm. If you allow your faith to be affected by your senses, you will be defeated in every encounter of life.

If, on the other hand, YOU ALLOW YOUR FAITH TO BE GOVERNED ONLY BY GOD'S WORD, YOU CAN BE NOTHING LESS THAN A WINNER. PRAISE GOD!

Satan will shoot a pain to your body, and then a thought to your mind suggesting that you *are still sick.* At this point what you confess with your mouth will determine what you will have. *"For verily I say unto you, That whosoever shall say unto this mountain, Be thou removed, and be thou cast*

into the sea; and shall not doubt in his heart, but shall believe that those things which he saith shall come to pass; he
shall have whatsoever he saith" (Mark 11:23). If you confess
the pain and symptoms, that will give Satan the legal right
to enforce it upon you. On the other hand, if you confess
what THE WORD OF GOD SAYS about your condition, you
will have that.

Confess HEALING, and you will have it according to
Mark 11:24:

At this point someone will say, "Brother Price, if I say
that I feel well, when in fact I feel bad, wouldn't I be telling
a lie?"

You are absolutely right! If you said you feel well when
in fact you feel bad, you would be telling a lie. I am not saying for you to confess that you *feel good* when you *feel bad*.
I'm saying that you are to CONFESS WHAT THE WORD
SAYS — not what you feel.

Is God a liar?

Certainly not! Well, He was the one who said it, I didn't!
I Peter 2:24 said, ". . . *and with His Stripes ye were healed.*"
God is telling you that you are healed, your body is telling
you that you are sick. Who are you going to believe? Which-
ever one that you confess is what you will have.

We are not saying — as some will tell you — "there is
no sickness and disease. It's all a state of mind."

That's a *lie of Satan* to deceive you. If there was no such
thing as *sickness and disease,* don't you think that GOD of
all people would know that? And yet He said that Jesus took
our infirmities and bore our sickness.

How could that be true, if sickness doesn't exist? *I AM
NOT SAYING THAT SICKNESS IS NOT REAL. I AM
NOT SAYING THAT PAIN IS NOT REAL.*

You may be experiencing pain right now.

I am not talking about what we *see* or *feel* — only about
what we *believe.*

If I believe what the Word of God says and confess that
with my mouth, then I am not lying but telling the truth,
the whole truth, and nothing but the truth.

Can you see that? Can you see the difference?

Right in the face of pain you must confess that you believe that you're healed. You are making a *confession of*

faith at that time and not a confession of physical and visible fact.

If somebody asks you how you feel, don't tell them. You are under no obligation to tell anybody how you feel. Understand?

If someone says, "How do you feel? You sure don't look very well."

You may be feeling terrible. Don't tell them you *feel good* if you *feel bad*.

Instead confess and tell them what you believe. Say "Praise God, the Word of God says, I Peter 2:24, 'With his stripes I was healed' and II Corinthians 5:7, says, 'We walk by faith and not by sight,' so according to the WORD OF GOD, I believe that I am healed, and I'm doing fine! How about you?"

At that point you're not lying, you're telling the truth according to the Word of God. Now when physical evidence comes — the cancer disappears, the eyesight clears up, the tumor vanishes, etc., then you can say — "I am healed!"

Until the physical evidence comes your confession should be, "I believe I'm healed, examine the Word of God — it proves that I am!"

When physical evidence comes, then you can say, "I am healed, examine my body, it proves it!" Praise God!

I hope this explanation helps you to see the difference between saying, "I believe I'm healed," and saying, "I am healed."

11

What About Medication?

This has been a real problem for many people.

They say, "When I pray and make my claim to my physical healing, until the physical evidence comes, should I continue to take my medication?"

Before I answer that, let me ask you this question. Does wearing glasses heal bad eyes? Does taking insulin heal diabetes? Does taking glycerine heal heart conditions? Does taking dyalisis heal kidneys?

You know as well as I do, that they don't. Wearing glasses doesn't heal bad eyes. If it did all you would have to do is wear glasses, you wouldn't even have to pray. But you know that *that* doesn't work like that — does it? Therefore, wearing glasses, taking glycerine, taking insulin, will not heal anything, and is therefore irrelevant, and immaterial to your healing. Whether you take medication or not has nothing at all to do with your healing, *unless your faith is in the medication.* If it is, and you stop taking it, then you are in serious trouble.

Remember that you are receiving your healing by faith. It is a matter of of what you believe in your heart, or spirit. Your heart — by faith — knows that you are healed, but your body doesn't know it *yet,* therefore, *it,* your body, may still need the medication, so go ahead and *take it if you need it.* All that the glasses and medication are doing is allowing the body to function at a normal level, until the physical healing is manifested in your body.

Now understand, if you had *a healing manifested in your body* and you continued in the face of that healing to take the medication, then that would be a denial of your healing, and would open the door for Satan and demons to put that same thing on you or something worse. If you are in fact healed, you don't need any medication, do you? But, when you are making a *stand in faith,* your body may still need the medication — and thank God it is available. Don't get in bondage, take the medication *if you need it.* If you can do without it — that's even better, because it will allow you to put your confidence in your faith, instead of the medication.

When "Gifts of Healings" operate or *miracle healings* as they are sometimes referred to, they are usually *instantaneous,* and therefore, there is no further need for glasses, crutches, wheelchairs, insulin, etc. But *faith healing* is different, most of the time. There can be a time factor between the time you pray and the time the physical evidence comes, and you may need the medication.

If you do — take it. It is not a denial of your faith. After all, remember that you have received your healing according to GOD'S WORD — not according to taking medication.

Many make the mistake of trying to prove that *faith healing* is *true* by not taking medication, instead of by the *clearly revealed WORD OF THE LIVING GOD.* If you said, "I'm healed!", and you kept on taking medication, that would look contradictory. If someone said to you, "I thought you said that you were healed!"

And you answered, "I am!"

They would say, "If you were healed, you wouldn't need medicine would you?"

There would be nothing that you could say.

BUT IF YOU SAID, "I BELIEVE THAT I AM," that would be a *statement of faith* — not of an accomplished fact. I hope you can see the difference.

PRAISE GOD! HEALING IS FOR ALL!

For a complete list of tapes and books
by Fred Price, or to receive his
publication, *Ever Increasing Faith
Messenger*, write:

Frederick K.C. Price
Crenshaw Christian Center
P. O. Box 90000
Los Angeles, CA 90009

*Feel free to include your prayer requests
and comments when you write.*

Books by Fred Price

HIGH FINANCE
God's Financial Plan
Tithes and Offerings

Now Faith Is

How Faith Works
(also available in Spanish)

Is Healing For All?

How To Obtain Strong Faith
Six Principles

The Holy Spirit — The Missing Ingredient

Faith, Foolishness, or Presumption?

Thank God For Everything?

Available at your local bookstore.

Harrison House
P.O. Box 35035 • Tulsa, OK 74153